THE GLUTEN-FREE GUIDE FOR SOUTHERN AFRICA

This edition is dedicated
to the beloved memory of
Matthew Joseph Hart
and written in the spirit
of his social commitment

The Gluten-free Guide for Southern Africa

Carole Smollan

Delta Books · Johannesburg

Originally published by the author 1975
Reprinted 1978, 1982, twice in 1992, 1994

This edition published in 1997 by
Delta Books
A DIVISION OF JONATHAN BALL PUBLISHERS (PTY) LTD
P O Box 33977
Jeppestown 2043

ISBN 0 908387 76 8

Design by Michael Barnett, Johannesburg
Typesetting and reproduction of cover by RT Sparhams (Pty) Ltd, Johannesburg
Typesetting and reproduction of text by Book Productions, Pretoria
Printed by National Book Printers, Drukkery Road, Goodwood, Western Cape

Contents

Acknowledgements

The development of this book over the years, could not have evolved without the wonderful support and encouragement of my two lovely 'glutenoid' daughters Tanya and Andrea. A special thank you to my son Daniel for his patience with a life that was largely 'pizza and pasta free'.

Sincere thanks to Leonard Ettlinger for all the years he *shlepped* gluten-free products back and forth and to our friends Emil Jackson and Shelley Gordon for happily eating gluten-free food with us.

My heartfelt appreciation to the doctors who gave their valuable insight, met their deadlines with such good grace and understood the need for information.

I am continually grateful to all my loyal suppliers who have done so much to alleviate the problems associated with this condition.

To the many loyal readers of previous editions of this book, the letters you have sent sharing your experiences have been invaluable.

And lastly, my thanks to Francine Blum, the project co-ordinator, for understanding the importance of the project.

FOREWORD

I would like to congratulate Carole Smollan on the publication of the long awaited revised edition of her book.

Gluten is an ubiquitous ingredient in our modern diet and often comes hidden in other foodstuffs. The successful treatment of gluten intolerance rests on the total withdrawal of gluten from the diet. This can be a daunting task for an individual and especially for a mother who has to find alternatives to keep a child on a totally gluten-free diet.

We are therefore fortunate to have Carole who has a long personal experience with gluten enteropathy and has raised her children with the condition. To this she brings a vast acquired knowledge on the subject, resulting in an informed, practical, usable book which should be indispensable to anybody who has a child with coeliac disease or individuals who are gluten intolerant or suspect that they may be intolerant.

Dr. Alta Smit MB BCH B Sc (Phys)

Author's Note

Dear Reader

Welcome to the seventh edition of *The Gluten-Free Guide for Southern Africa.*

Over 23 years and 6 editions the little 'glutenoids', as our friends call my children, have grown up and left home. I was very gratified to hear, that on arrival in a new country, the first thing they did was to contact the coeliac societies and manufacturers to obtain lists of gluten-free foods to immediately make their lives easier, safer and healthier by being aware of exactly what local products they could eat with absolute confidence. All the years of quiet insistence on 'checking labels' had actually won through.

Any new lifestyle tends to be stressful and more demanding. As a coeliac, always try to put aside extra resting time for yourself.

Remember the 'coeliac circle', as I call it. If your body gets tired your system does not operate in top gear and your absorption rate is likely to drop. As you already suffer from malabsorption, (you absorb less nutrients than your non-coeliac neighbour), this is not an ideal situation, and you should always try to remain healthy in a well-planned way.

Facilities for a gluten-free diet are growing broader worldwide. Until the last decade gluten was not easily recognised as a major factor in food intolerances, whereas it is now top of the list in both Britain and America. TV programmes and lectures are becoming more and more common. Gluten-free products are becoming more abundant and easily available.

A coeliac mother has to make considerable effort during the early years to make her children comfortable with the fact that their food is not simple 'take-away food' and to make it a natural part of their lives to plan ahead. But the rewards are significant and the task is becoming easier and more manageable as the product range expands.

Never feel embarrassed to ask about ingredients. You are entitled to eat safely and you alone should be responsible for your own welfare.

Bon Appetit. Make your gluten-free diet a 'positive' factor in your life.

Carole Smollan

Understanding Your Condition

Introduction

Gluten is a sticky protein found in many grains. However, only in wheat, rye, oats and barley is it harmful to the small intestine when coeliac disease is present.

Gluten provides the structure for baked foods by giving them a pliable and elastic texture. Without the gluten baked foods look flat and do not rise properly.

If you have a friend or relative who needs a gluten-free diet, please understand that a gluten-free diet is not a choice, it is a medical necessity and it has to be 100% gluten-free. It is important not only to eliminate all gluten-free foods from your diet, but also to adequately replace the carbohydrates in your daily diet to provide energy and all round nutrition.

When you suspect gluten as the catalyst for your intolerance, it is important NOT to experiment with a gluten-free diet before the biopsy as this can affect a correct result being obtained. Blood tests cannot, with certainty, indicate coeliac disease, but can determine whether or not a biopsy should be performed.

Arthritis, anaemia, inexplicable malnutrition, Sjogrens syndrome, Graves disease, Attention Deficit Disorder and auto-immune diseases are some of the indications that could implicate investigation for coeliac disease.

The Medical Viewpoint

Over the last decade diagnostic facilities for coeliac disease have shortened the period of investigation considerably. I have chosen five specialist doctors to present a simple explanation for you the reader.

As you will see from the following pages, good communication with your medical team, proper and complete reporting of symptoms by the patient to the doctor, will go a long way to speed up the process of correctly diagonising disease where the symptoms can be largely non-specific.

Adult Coeliac Desease

Coeliac disease is a hereditary disorder of the immune system in which ingestion of gluten in foods containing wheat, rye, oats and barley, leads to damage of the small intestinal mucosa. This results in malabsorption of nutrients and vitamins.

In recent years it has become evident that the condition is more prevalent than previously believed and is frequently underdiagnosed, particularly in adults who may present with subtle symptoms.

If left untreated coeliac disease may result in serious complications including anaemia, bone disease and gastrointestinal malignancy. Early recognition is therefore important since these complications can be prevented by adherence to a gluten-free diet.

Although the condition usually manifests in the first few years of life following the introduction of cereals into the diet, over 50% of cases present for the first time in adulthood. In adults the symptoms may be highly varied and range from severe weight loss and diarrhoea with bulky offensive stools, to subtle complaints of cramp, abdominal bloating, flatulence and even constipation. These individuals are often erroneously diagnosed as having an irritable bowel syndrome. Recurrent oral aphthous ulcers are common and should arouse suspicion of the condition.

Approximately half the amount of adults with coeliac disease will have no gastrointestinal symptoms whatsoever but will present with complications of nutrient malabsorption. The most common complaints are anaemia resulting from iron and folic acid deficiency, osteoporosis resulting from calcium and Vitamin D deficiency, menstrual irregularity and neurological disorders including muscle weakness and pre-senile dementia due to multiple nutrient deficiencies. The development of early osteoarthritis may also be a pointer to the condition.

Dermatitis herpetiformis is a variant of coeliac disease in which clusters of itchy blisters occur, usually over the buttocks, knees and elbows. This also responds to withdrawal of gluten from the diet.

At present small intestinal mucosal biopsy remains the

cornerstone for diagnosis and coeliac disease should never be diagnosed without performing this procedure. The procedure is safe and is usually performed at the time of gastrointestinal endoscopy. Blood tests such as the antigliadin antibodies and antiendomysial antibodies have been introduced over the past few years but none have shown 100% accuracy in diagnosing the condition. These tests are limited by expense and are currently available in only certain centres in South Africa.

It must be remembered that not everybody presented with the above complaints will have coeliac disease, but greater awareness of the symptoms will certainly help meet the challenge of early diagnosis and management of this very treatable disorder. The dietary principles outlined by Carole Smollan in the following pages also go a long way to achieving this goal.

Michael Strimling
Gastroenterologist
Johannesburg

Homeopathic Overview

Food intolerance is becoming more and more recognised as the cause for the vast array of symptoms we see in modern, industrialised man. Doctors are often confounded by a number of seemingly unrelated symptoms ranging from behavioural to systemic to localised gut symptoms which cannot be put under the umbrella of one particular disease. Gluten induced enteropathy is probably one of the best described of these intolerance syndromes, although in its milder forms it often goes unrecognised in many individuals as there are degrees to which the gut and the rest of the body are affected.

What is gluten enteropathy?

Gluten enteropathy is a condition where the lining of the gut or the epithelial layer develops a reaction to the alphagliadin portion of gluten, the protein found in wheat, oats, barley (including malt) and rye. The lining then responds with inflammation with the result that the lining becomes thinner and eventually the folds of the gut will become flat. New evidence suggests that gluten intolerance would also cause the tight junctions between the lining cells to pull apart, thus rendering the gut more 'leaky' or permeable to other toxins.

Because 80% of our immune system lies in the gut, just beyond the lining, the immune cells will be activated and these can get into the bloodstream and cause inflammation in other parts of the body, explaining the symptoms such as joint pain and skin conditions such as dermatitis herpetiformis (a skin rash with blisters) as well as local bowel symptoms in response to gluten.

The liver, being our second line of defence, becomes overloaded and cannot process other environmental toxins. Symptoms such as behavioural disturbances, mood swings, depression and headaches may be the result of this. The gut-friendly bacteria also suffer and bad strains of bacteria may overgrow causing bloating and more toxins to be absorbed. Lastly, because the integrity of the lining cells is impaired they cannot digest certain foodstuffs or absorb certain key nutrients like vitamins and minerals, with the result that malabsorption occurs. This will result in severe cases in large bubbly stools, the symptoms of vitamin and mineral deficiency and anaemia.

As a result of this the individual may also develop other food intolerances such as lactose intolerance because the enzyme which processes lactose is disturbed and a further increase in the symptoms will occur.

The first line of treatment is the complete removal of gluten and sometimes also dairy products from the diet. Support for the bowel in the form of herbal extracts, certain vitamins, amino acids and evening primrose oil help to regenerate the lining once the inflammation has subsided.

Dr Alta Smit MB BCH BSC (PHYS)

Coeliac Disease in Children

Coeliac disease is one of a group of illnesses caused by food intolerance. It was originally included with severe diseases called Chronic Intestinal Indigestion (CCI).

With the Nazi occupation of Holland during World War II all the wheat of that country was sent to Germany. It was noticed that due to the lack of wheat in their diet, children who had been labelled as having CCI improved considerably – and deteriorated again, post-war, when wheat once again became available. As a result of this observation gluten was eventually identified as the cause of CCI in 1950. CCI was renamed Coeliac Disease or Gluten Induced Enteropathy. It soon became apparent that the harmful substance in gluten was the gliadin fraction and that some form of immune mechanism was at work in the causation of this illness. There is also clear evidence of a genetic influence, in that there is a high incidence of asymptomatic coeliac disease as determined by intestinal biopsy in first-degree relatives of children with coeliac disease.

The pathological features that make up coeliac disease have been defined mainly by biopsy specimens obtained from the duodenum and the upper part of the small intestine, known as the jejunum. The most typical appearance is called total villous atrophy. This means that the finger-like processes which are so important in the digestive processes occurring in the small intestine are completely absent. This damage may not always be complete, but even in these rarer cases the villi are shortened and widened.

The symptoms of coeliac disease do not develop until gluten-containing foods are introduced into the infants' diet. In many cases the symptoms are first noticed after the ninth month of life, but the child is often not seen by a paediatrician until the second year. A considerable number of mild cases go undetected for much longer, even into adult life.

It is important to realise that if wheat-containing cereals are introduced into the diet of infants at a very early age, coeliac disease may appear in the first nine months of life.

The first symptom is usually a personality change and the child becomes irritable and miserable. The appetite is very poor and there is failure to gain weight. Stools are noted to be porridgy in consistency and are pale, bulky and foul-smelling – these features may not be present in all cases. In some children the illness may start with vomiting and diarrhoea and this is often thought in error to be due to gastroenteritis. The child's abdomen becomes distended due to the fermentation of carbohydrates in foods and this contrasts with the obvious wasting of the child's buttocks and thighs. As a result of calcium deprivation bones may become brittle and growth is delayed.

Other abnormalities include anaemia due to iron-deficiency, deficiency in vitamin B complex and in rare occasions deficiency in both vitamins A and D.

A wide variety of screening tests have been developed down the years. These include fat balance studies, xylose tolerance tests and a range of newer immunological tests. However, the diagnosis of coeliac disease is only acceptable when it is based on the characteristic appearance of the small intestinal (jejunal) biopsy.

The treatment of coeliac disease is based on its recognition as a gluten-induced intestinal disorder. The results of treatment with a gluten-free diet are impressive. This is first noted as a striking improvement in the personality of the child followed by rapid growth. The stools slowly return to normal. Satisfactory results require a great sense of responsibility on the part of the parents who must adhere to their child's dietary requirements and teach their children to accept this in a responsible way.

An adequate intake of vitamins, especially vitamin D is important. The child should also receive an adequate amount of fruit every day. Iron-deficiency anaemia is prevented by taking adequate iron supplements. It is often useful to take extra folic acid on a daily basis as well.

As long as the child remains on a gluten-free diet, growth development will be normal. Pregnancy is often associated with relapses in previous coeliac disease sufferers. Other adults appear to have completely 'outgrown' their coeliac disease and can apparently eat a normal diet. However, these apparently healthy adults may have abnormally low levels of folic acid and iron in their bodies and anaemia may occur.

The abnormal pattern of the villous processes of the small intestine returns to normal with successful treatment but relapses if gluten is re-introduced into the diet. This relapse is accompanied by the recurrence of all the characteristic features of the illness.

Professor E G Weinberg
Paediatrician
Red Cross Childrens' Hospital, Cape Town

Coeliac Disease –
A Pathologist's Perspective

Malabsorption has been defined as any state in which there is a disturbance in the net absorption of any constituent across the intestinal mucosa. In coeliac disease the malabsorption is due to mucosal damage that is produced by a genetically determined cell-mediated abnormal immune response to gluten (hence the alternative name of gluten-sensitive enteropathy).

The normal villi of the small bowel (intestine) are tall and finger-shaped (Figure 1). This increases the absorptive surface of the bowel which enhances its absorptive capacity.

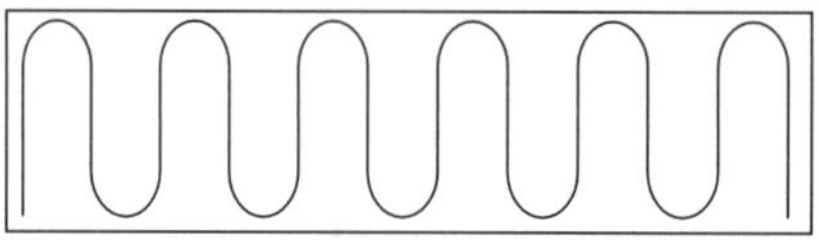

Figure 1 Healthy villi

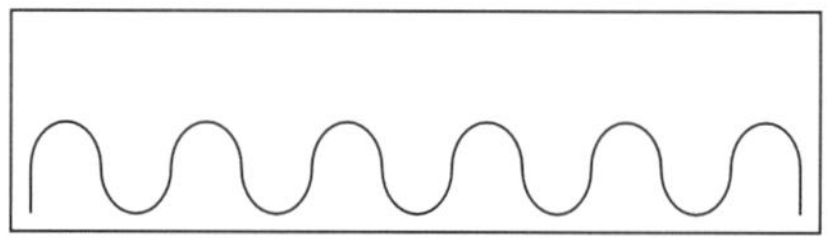

Figure 2 Flattened villi

Sensitivity to gluten results in the destruction of these villi leading to sub-total villous atrophy or flattening of the mucus (Figure 2). The villous atrophy is almost certainly due to premature destruction of cells known as enterocytes. The absorptive capacity of the small bowel is thus greatly diminished and this leads to malabsorption. The primary mucosal lesions are most severe in the upper part of the small intestine and become progressively less marked distally.

Although pathologists are able to measure increased faecal fat in the stools, assess lactose intolerance, and are able to detect anti-gliadin and anti-endomysial antibodies in the blood, the intestinal biopsy is still the primary diagnostic investigative procedure in this condition. Not only is the pathologist able to determine sub-total villous atrophy following gluten administration, but they are also able to determine a measurable improvement in villous architecture when gluten is withdrawn from the diet.

Apart from the changes to the villi, the pathologist is also able to notice increases of plasma cells in the mucosa and lymphocytes amidst the villous epithelial cells. The presence of these cells supports the immune nature of the disease process.

Pathologists recognise the skin condition known as dermatitis herpetiformis to co-exist with coeliac disease. Established associations between coeliac disease and diabetes mellitus, selective IgA deficiency, primary sclerosing cholangitis, primary biliary cirrhosis, ulcerative colitis and lymphocytic colitis have also been recognised.

Good communication between clinicians and pathologists is important in order to establish these associations. This communication is also essential as small intestine, tumours (especially lymphoma) as well as extra-intestinal malignancy (eg oesophageal carcinoma) may complicate coeliac disease. The entire team involved in the care of patients with coeliac disease can play a major role, not only in the management of the disease, but also in limiting the severity of all the complications.

Dr R B Skudowitz
Consultant Pathologist

Laboratory Tests for Allergy

Allergy testing is a practical way to discover to which foods you are allergic. However, none of the techniques available are 100% accurate; most are, at best, 60-70% accurate. Nonetheless, some method of pinpointing allergies is necessary and testing is a valuable part of the discovery process.

There are several different methods of allergy testing – some conventional, others most unconventional – which are carried out by doctors, clinics, laboratories and health practitioners. The method you choose really depends on what appeals to you, what you can afford, and what is available in your area. Some of the more commonly used tests are listed below. The more information you can gather yourself about the nature and frequency of your symptoms, suspect foods etc, the more efficient the results will be.

SPT and RAST tests measure the specific IgE (immunoglobulin E – antibody E) which is produced and which cause immediate (anaphylactic) reaction. These are typified by symptoms caused by the release of histamine excess mucous production (blocked nose) nerve ending stimulation (itch). Vasodilation swelling and redness smooth muscle contraction (broncho construction etc).

Skin Prick Tests are normally done by a nursing sister, trained in skin prick testing, at a laboratory or depot. Eight or nine commonly inhaled allergies are used for testing.

It is essential to establish if the patient is on any medication, eg oral cortisone, anti-histamines or mask, cell stabilisers.

In some practises the doctor has his own kit and is able to do the tests. The test is quick and easy to perform and takes about 20 minutes for the results to be read.

SPT is very cost effective and can be done with safety in a controlled environment where a qualified person is available in case of an emergency.

SPT is not recommended for patients under 3 years of age or over 55 years old.

SPT is also not recommended for foodstuff where reaction is highly potent (anaphylactic) eg peanuts.

RAST tests can only take place in a laboratory using special equipment. A sample is drawn at the doctor's rooms or at the laboratory and a multi-disc, consisting of approximately 18 commonly inhaled allergies, are tested for.

A paediatric food screening test, consisting of six foodstuffs, ie egg white, milk, wheat, peanuts, soya beans and white fish, is called FXJ. Both are recommended for children up to eight years of age.

The IgE mediated food allergies are normally outgrown by children at 10 years, but certain foods – peanuts, wheat, sea food allergies – seem to persist into adulthood.

There are over 400 allergens and these can be requested from any laboratory. However, it is more economical to be specific.

An added advantage of the blood test is that results can be obtained quantitatively to gauge the sensitivity of the patient.

Both SPT and RAST are fully re-imbursable by medical aids.

Patch tests are available at numerous specialised centres for delayed reaction sensitivity.

Once again, it is stressed that any diagnostic test cannot be taken on its own and is only part of the allergic jig-saw puzzle, where avoidance and elimination of the offending identifiable allergen is essential.

Maria Ramsay
Laboratory Specialities cc

Elimination Diets

This is one of the most reliable ways of detecting food allergies. It involves taking one or more foods out of the diet for at least seven days, and then reintroducing the eliminated foods, one at a time, to watch for an adverse reaction. During the exclusion period, any substances which are affecting the system adversely will be eliminated from the body. If your symptoms improve or, better still, disappear during this time, then you can be fairly sure that a food allergy is causing your problems.

One of the best things about elimination diets is that they unmask hidden allergies. Generally, after five days, the body is free of the offending foods and becomes hypersensitive, so that when trigger foods are reintroduced there is a marked and definite reaction, which leaves no doubt as to the cause. Often, a favourite food can be a trigger without being obvious.

For some people it will take longer than seven days for food to leave their system. Others can have delayed reactions of up to forty-eight hours, which makes the reintroduction of foods a lengthy process and which could cause nutritional deficiencies. Anyone who embarks on an elimination diet needs to be aware of the commitment that such a rigorous régime demands and of the need to be thorough and medically supervised. On the other hand, you will feel an enormous sense of achievement when you discover an allergen.

Keeping a food diary of your daily intake will clarify the picture for you.

Example:

TIME	FOOD EATEN	BRAND NAME	REACTION

NEW DIAGNOSTIC TESTS ON THE HORIZON

There are a number of diagnostic procedures currently being investigated:

Antigliadin antibody tests (AGA)
This test has the potential for useful screening but does not as yet replace the small bowel biopsy.

Fast breath hydrogen
Saliva testing
Fingerprinting
Dental screening

All are showing possibilities but are not currently available.

Skin tests are available for allergies such as sniffing, sneezing, snorting or coughing, headaches, sinus, abdominal pains and nausea. All these symptoms could be an ongoing problem, and often you doctor will order tests to try and gain a direction as to what the cause could be.

Is it an allergy?

This is the answer we need to have when seeking the solution. Diagnostic tests, as with all tests, are only accurate if the correct test is done for the correct problem on the correct patient.

The two most common tests at the moment are:
SPT an in vivo Skin Prick test
RAST an in vitro blood test.

Both have been around for a while and have their applications in the market. It is important to remember that no diagnostic test is accurate, or complete, without a full and comprehensive patient case history as well as all the other factors of the patient's environment – home and work, hobbies, indoors and outdoors.

Once the complete picture has been established and the history confirms the diagnosis, a practical plan for eliminating the source of the problem can be devised. In the case of a wheat intolerance being indicated, the possibility of coeliac disease or dermatitis herpetiformis can further be investigated.

Associated Conditions

Coeliac disease is part of an auto immune deficiency, and as such, is linked to several other conditions which are often seen, in conjunction with coeliac disease.

Here we discuss the more common conditions. There are, however, many more, such as Hashimoto's disease, Addison's disease, Lupus and Sjogrens syndrome.

LACTOSE INTOLERANCE AND/OR COW'S MILK PROTEIN INTOLERANCE

Approximately 24% of coeliacs are also lactose intolerant. I have found that patients who have been on a gluten-free diet for some time and whose digestive systems have settled down often experience an improvement in their ability to digest lactose.

Lactose intolerance means that the mucous membrane of the small intestine has an insufficient level of the enzyme, lactase, to break down milk sugar. These symptoms usually manifest shortly after the intake of milk products. However, congenital lactose intolerance, although rare, has been documented. This is the reaction to the milk sugar in breast milk.

Lactose intolerance may also be indicated where, due to medication, intestinal infection or post-operative intestinal trauma, the lactase activity is reduced and this may remain as a permanent situation.

A lactose intolerance test is available, where a lactose solution is drunk followed by the taking of blood samples in order to measure how efficiently the milk sugar is broken down in the intestine.

In the general population it is normal that on weaning, the body will stop producing the enzymes needed to digest milk, and if one lives in a society where milk products are not commonly eaten, the ability to digest lactose disappears, eg in eastern or chinese cuisine. Some populations developed the genetic ability to continue producing a small amount of lactase. I have found that most people with lactose intolerance cheat on a regular basis – a bit of chocolate, medication containing lactose (HRT or contraception), just a bit of cheese cake, to hell with the consequences. Consequently, these people continue to produce a small amount of the enzyme lactase, and this gives rise to the report in the British Medical Journal that lactose intolerant people can tolerate a small amount of lactose per day.

This directive cannot include people with cow's milk protein intolerance and here I speak from my own experience. This produces a much harsher reaction, exhibiting symptoms such as cramps, vomiting, diarrhoea, colic, rashes, hay fever, eczema and even a few long term effects such as arthritis and rheumatoid problems.

People with cow's milk intolerance should have NO milk products, and if this régime is strictly followed, symptoms should be absent.

However, it also means that lactase will no longer be required by the body and thus the enzyme will no longer be required in the intestine.

Calcium can be found in many products other than milk products and care should be taken to include these in your daily diet to compensate.

Alternative forms of calcium rich foods are:

sesame seeds	beans
tahina	nuts
sea vegetables	broccoli
kelp and agar	parsley

Food labels can be very confusing as they sometimes use alternative words and phrases to describe lactose. eg milk products, milk solids, whey, whey powder, milk sugar, curd, casein, galactose, milk sugar and skim milk powder.

There is at present very little documented about lactose intolerance. I, Carole Smollan, have been travelling the world as well as surfing the Net to research the differing conditions recognised by various cultures for inclusion in my new publication on hypolactasia (lactose intolerance).

If you are lactose intolerant it would be very helpful to me if you would kindly send me your name and address on a postcard. My details are at the back of this book.

DERMATITIS HERPETIFORMIS

This is a rare and intensely itchy condition in which patients develop a cutaneous eruption consisting of patches of weals, bumps or blisters varying in size from small to large. The eruption is usually symmetrical. The majority of patients have a gluten-induced bowel abnormality which may not produce symptoms.

Dematitis herpetiformis occurs mainly between the ages of 20 to 55 years. Males are affected twice as frequently as females. The condition may occur gradually or suddenly and itching is usually the first symptom. The distribution of the lesions is characteristic – the front of the knees, the outside surface of the elbows and the buttocks. The shoulders, body, face and scalp are also frequently involved.

The disease runs a very long course with exacerbations and remissions. In about one third of the patients the symptoms gradually become less troublesome and there may be prolonged periods of improvement or apparent cure.

The diagnosis is made by means of a biopsy of an affected area which is sent for pathological examination, and a specific immunofluorescent test.

The treatment requires an oral medication, dapsone or alternatively sulphupynodine if diapsone cannot be tolerated. Because at least two-thirds of the patients have a gluten related bowel abnormality, a strict gluten-free diet may not only improve the enteropathy but also reduce the diapsone dose and in some cases the diapsone can be stopped.

Dr Barbara Goldberg
Dermatologist
Johannesburg

Diabetic Coeliac

Coping with a restriction of both gluten and sugar is doubly difficult. It is important to maintain both diets correctly but the coeliac diet must be managed as 100% gluten-free and the diabetic diet worked around it. Fructose is gluten-free. The carbohydrates in your diet must be modified to maintain diabetic control.

Vitamin Supplements

For best results space supplements as evenly as possible throughout the day. If you require two or more doses of any particular supplement per day, take one in the morning and one after your evening meal for maximum benefit. Some supplements, especially calcium, are best taken in the evening when mineral fluid flux in the body is highest. If you like taking your supplements all at once, do so after your evening meal.

Time release products may be beneficial in encouraging optimum and steady blood levels.

Counteract the poor absorption of nutrients. Glucose-intolerant sufferers need to supplement their regular diets. The Vital Multitime range of multivitamins are available in special formulas to meet the differing needs of children, women, and active adults. New to the range are Multitime for over 45's, Multitime for Teens and Multitime for Sportspeople.

When travelling, take all necessary medication along with you to be confident in the knowledge that the ingredients have been checked.

Medication and Pharmaceuticals

Strange as it may seem, many pharmaceuticals contain both/either lactose or gluten. At present there is no legislation that compels the manufacturers to publish a list of ingredients.

I have provided a basic list of off-the-shelf pharmaceuticals which are gluten-free. In other cases, please ask your pharmacist to check the manufacturing company, as knowledge of which drugs contain gluten or lactose is uncommon. Please remember that ingredients may vary from pills to syrups or other mediums. Always read labels as contents change on a regular basis.

I have found that a vitamin B injection once a year is very beneficial to coeliacs in order to catch up a little with malabsorption. It might be a good idea to discuss this with your doctor.

Constipation

If you started out as a coeliac with diarrhoea it might be that in later years this will be replaced by constipation.

Chronic constipation is a symptom that is often missed in diagnosis. Try adding fibre to your gluten-free diet which is already lower in fibre than a normal balanced diet.

Eat a helping of raw grated carrots for breakfast, add dried apricots and prunes to your baking. Use whole grains, lentils, peas and raisins as often as possible. Try some of the new vegetable juices and exercise regularly. Raise the level of your fitness.

Gluten and Lactose-free Products from Bioforce

Acne Formula
Allergy Formula
Anti-appetite Formula
Arthritis Formula
Asthma Formula
Bladder Irritation Formula
Cellulitis Formula
Circulation Formula
Cold Formula
Concentration Formula
Echinaforce
Ecxzema Formula
Helix Slim
Haemorrhoid Formula
Immunoforce
Indigestion Formula
Infuaforce
Liver and Gallbladder Formula
Menopause Formula
Menstruation Formula
Nervous-insomnia Formula
Neuroforce Formula
Pollinosan Liquid Formula
Prostate Formula
Rheumatism Formula
Sinus Formula
Varicose Veins Formula

These products are available from pharmacies and health shops. For more information phone the toll-free helpline on 0800-111 570.

Gluten- and Lactose-free Products from Sportron International Products

- Completron
- Completron Junior
- Neurotron
- Circutron
- Respitron
- Respitron Syrup
- Ultragard
- Omegatone
- Aloe Vera Juice
- Digestron
- Femtron
- Gentron
- A-tron
- Promin
- Calcitone
- Infagard
- Sportron Herbal Tea

Gluten-free Products from Abbott Laboratories

- Advera
- Alitraq
- Ensure
  (Chocolate, natural, strawberry, vanilla)
- Glucerna
- Isomil
- Jenty
- Osmolite
- Osmolite HN
- Pediasure
- Pulmocare
- Suplena
- Vital

Initially when one is diagnosed with a gluten intolerance, or at times, post-operatively, the body needs a simply absorbed method of nutrition. Ensure is an excellent gluten and lactose-free remedy.

Gluten and Lactose-free Products from Rhone-Poulenc Rorer (SA)

Adrenalin (1ml injection)
Allomaron tablets
Anethaine cream
Anthisan (50 and 100mg tablets)
Anthisan elixir
Anthisan (2ml injection)
Anthisan cream
Arsobal injection
Ascablol emulsion
Biovital tonic
Brolene eye ointment
Brolene eye drops
Bronchicough elixir
Bronchicum pastilles
Bronchiflu syrup
Bronchistop
Cerubidin
Clexane 40
Depuran capsules
Dequacets
Dequamed
Dequadin mouth paint
Dequadin oral antiseptic
Dequadin throat lozenges
Emetrol oral solution
Essaven capsules
Essaven gel
Essentiale ampoules
Essentiale capsules
Felixir syrup
Flagyl (200 tablets)
Flagyl (400 tablets)
Flagyl injection
Flagyl (500mg and 1g suppositories)
Flaxedil (2ml injection)
Gardenal sodium injection
Garoin tablets
Halothane anaesthetic gas
Intraval sodium powder for solution
Isofor anaesthetic gas
Largactil ampoules
Largactil injection
Lipostabil capsules
Maalox plus suspension
Maalox plus tablets
Maalox tablets
Maalox extra strength tablets
Microphyllin (60 mg capsules)
Microphyllin (125mg capsules)
Microphyllin (250mg capsules)
Myocrisin (50mg injection)
Nasacor
Neulactil (2.5 and 10 mg tablets)
Nivaquine injection
Nivaquine tablets
Nivaquine syrup
Orucote suppositories
Orudis 50 mg capsules
Orudis 100 mg capsules
Oruvail (100mg capsules)
Oruvail (200mg capsules)
Pentacarinat (300mg)
Phenergan cream
Phenergan elixir
Phenergan injection
Phensedyl
Piportil depot injection
Posterisan ointment
Posterisan suppositories

Secadrex tablets
Sectral (100mg and 200mg capsules)
Sectral (400mg tablets)
Stemetil (5mg tablets)
Stemetil injection
Stemetil syrup
Sulphadiazine injection
Suplena
Surmontil (10mg and 25mg tablets)
Surmontil (50mg capsules)
Tixylix linctus
Vallergan forte syrup

The following preparations contain lactose:
Avomine tablets
Largactil (10, 25, 50 and 100mg tablets)
Orucote (50mg and 100 mg tablets)
Phenergan (10mg and 25mg tablets)

Gluten- and Lactose-free Products from G G Searle

Canderel sachets
Canderel S F S
Efadin
Efamol G
Efamol Marine
Equal Sachets
Metamucil

Gluten- and Lactose-free Products from Amino Research

Digestive Enzyme Products

L-Actizyme – Dairy food digestant
Beano-Complex carbohydrate digestive enzyme
Super enzyme – Enzyme formula

Specialised Imported Vitamins and Minerals

A large range of vitamin and mineral products

Specialised Hyper-allergenic Protein Beverages

Ultracare for kids
Ultracare for adults

Potency-guaranteed Friendly-bacteria Products by Natren®

Milk-free Acidophilus Powder
Bifidonate Dairy-free Powder
Life Start for babies and children

Telephone (011) 4428242
Fax (011) 4428225

GLUTEN- AND LACTOSE-FREE PRODUCTS FROM ROCHE PHARMACEUTICALS

AAA spray
Aircol cream
Alcobon tabs
Anapolon tabs
Aspro clear
Bactrim DS tabs
Bactrim IV
Bactrim tabs
Cal-C-Vita
Dalmadorm
Dynajets
Histalix syrup
Konakion (10ml amps)
Lomudal aerosol
Lomudol inhaler
Madopar tabs
Naprosyn (250ml EC tabs/ 500 EC tabs)
Naprosyn 500mg tabs
Naprosyn S/R tabs
Natulan caps
Pevaryl
Pevaryl spray
Pexatron 250mg/500mg
Redoxon
Rennie peppermint/spearmint
Sanatogen antioxid
Sanatogen for children
Sanatogen multi and iron
Sanatogen vit C
Supradyn N E F tabs
Synflex
Tilcotil EF tabs
Valium amps

GLUTEN-FREE BUT CONTAIN LACTOSE

Dormicum 15 tabs/7.5 tabs
Flourouracil caps
Hivid 0.375 tabs
Lexotan 3 tabs/6 tabs
Librium 25 ml tabs
Mogadon tabs
Mucocaps
Mucocaps forte
Primperan tabs
Sanatogen powder regular
Sanatogen vit E
Supradyn NSC tabs
Valium 2 tabs/ 5 tabs
Valium 10 tabs

Gluten and Lactose-free Products from Adcock Ingram

ADCO GENERICS

Adco - Acyclovir topical cream
Adco - Amoxycillin 125mg/5ml suspension
Adco - Amoxycillin 250mg/5ml suspension
Adco - Atenolol 50 and 100mg tablets
Adco - Bromazepam 3 and 6mg tablets
Adco - Calcium chloride 10% injection
Adco - Cephalexin 250mg capsules
Adco - Cephalexin 125mg/5ml suspension
Adco - Cephalexin 250mg/5ml suspension
Adco - Clotrimazole topical cream
Adco - Clotrimazole vaginal cream
Adco - Co-Trimoxazole tablets
Adco - Co-Trimoxazole adult and paediatric tablets
Adco - Cyclizine syrup
Adco - Dextrose injection 500mg/ml
Adco - Diclofenac 75mg/3ml injection
Adco - Diclofenac 25 and 50mg tablets
Adco - Dol syrup
Adco - Dol tablets
Adco - Erythromycin 125mg/5ml suspension
Adco - Ethyl chloride spray
Adco - Flupain syrup
Adco - Furosemide 40mg tablets
Adco - Indomethacin 25mg capsules
Adco - Indomethacin gel
Adco - Loperamide syrup
Adco - Loten tablets
Adco - Magnesium 50% m/v injection
Adco - Mannitol 25% m/v injection
Adco - Mebendazole suspension
Adco - Mefenamic acid 250mg capsules
Adco - Methylene blue 1% injection
Adco - Methyl dopa 200mg and 500mg tablets
Adco - Metronidazole 200mg and 400mg tablets
Adco - Muco expec syrup

Adco - Naloxone injection 0,4mg/ml
Adco - Nystatin suspension
Adco - Nystatin vaginal cream
Adco - Phenobarbitone vitalet elixir
Adco - Piroxicam 10mg and 20mg capsules
Adco - Potassium chloride 15% m/v injection
Adco - Propranol 10,40 and 80mg and 160mg tablets
Adco - Quinine dihydrochloride 300mg/ml
Adco - Sinal tablets
Adco - Sinal co tablets
Adco - Sodium bicarbonate injection 4%
Adco - Sodium Bicarbonate injection 8.5%
Adco - Sodium Chloride injection 20%
Adco - Sodium Chloride injection 0.9%
Adco - Sterile water diluent injection
Adco - Sufedrin syrup
Adco - Tussend syrup
Adco - Vitamin B CO injection
Adco - Vitamin B12 injection
Remicaine 2% ampoule injection
Remicaine 1% vial injection
Remicaine 2% vial injection
Remicard injection
Topical jelly

Taking Control – Lifestyle Management

Helpful Hints for Coeliacs

The best way to have a healthy diet, within the gluten-free limitations, is to eat as broad a selection of foods as can be found in your area. This way you will obtain a cross-section of most of the minerals and vitamins you require.

For people who cheat or give up on the gluten-free diet, it can take as long as two years for obvious symptoms to reappear, but during that time you will have done untold damage. In some cases the reaction can be immediate.

The diet discussed in this book requires extra iron and folic acid, so ensure that you include leafy green vegetables in your diet. At the onset, these may cause flatulence, but as your system begins to operate correctly, your digestion will settle down and these items will become an important part of your natural food intake.

To obtain natural fibre I eat grated carrots every day, raisins and dried apples, nuts and seeds. Apple cider is lovely for those missing a beer! 'Hot' apple cider with cinnamon is delicious in winter (Hunters Gold).

Be aware of the commodities in your kitchen. The easiest and safest route is to have two toasters, as the wheat bread toast could put crumbs onto your gluten-free toast. Check your butter dish, toaster, bread slicer, bread board and griller.

Keep separate bread tins.

Lastly, trust your own judgement. If you have a reaction check back over everything that you have eaten, and where you ate it. Any new product should be carefully investigated, so that you do not repeat the ingestion of gluten. If you try hard enough, you will find the gluten that caused your discomfort.

Did You Know?

Coeliac disease means a gluten-free diet for life. The belief that the condition can be outgrown has long been dismissed.

A trial gluten-free diet can seriously interfere with a definite diagnosis from a small intestinal biopsy as your villi may improve sufficiently to misrepresent the outcome.

Some coeliacs may have a questionable reaction to a gluten-free diet, particularly at the beginning. Please persevere to allow your system time to settle down.

The absence of diarrhoea does not preclude a diagnosis of coeliac disease. Sixty-four percent of coeliacs in America are diagnosed with anaemia and lack of folic acid. Constipation is also common as is numbness in the fingertips, nausea and bone pain.

Coeliacs tend to tire more quickly than people whose absorption rate is higher. This is sometimes a problem in teenagers who do not accept their limitations.

Coeliac disease is a family problem. Family members should be aware of the other members in the family who have a lesser degree of gluten tolerance.

Ulcerative colitis and Crohn's disease are sometimes included in the same studies, as their symptoms can be similar.

You should not use malt-based vinegar.

Wheat germ oil used continuously, as in a shampoo, is not a good idea.

Mixed or vegetable cooking oils could well include wheat germ oil. Stick to pure sunflower seed or olive oil.

Do not lick stamps or envelopes. The glue usually contains gluten.

ALCOHOL

Grain derived alcohol is a problem. Beer and whisky are also not recommended. The distillation process is supposed to remove the gluten, but many coeliacs still report a reaction. Write to the manufacturers and research your favourite drink.

Wine, rum, tequila and saki are usually safe. Some vodkas are in order, but if you experience a reaction you will know not to try that brand again.

Liqueurs may be made with grain alcohol and are suspect. Bourbon, rye and gin are forbidden.

Settle for apple cider. It also makes a great sauce for casseroles and stews.

Malt is produced by steeping barley in water and heating. The resulting malt is not gluten-free. Malt extract is obtained from malted barley using a process where only water soluble products appear in the final extract. As gluten is insoluble in water, the resulting malt is gluten-free.

Communion Wafers

The Italian Coeliac Society has made representation to the Pope to make alternative arrangements for people needing gluten-free wafers, particularly priests and children. A decision is pending. Please discuss this with your minister, as repeatedly eating biscuits containing wheat will be harmful.

The Controversy About Oats and Rye

Oats and rye are of different families to wheat, and therefore do not produce the same harsh effect on coeliacs as ingesting wheat does. However, American research has indicated that oats and rye can still affect the villi over a longer and less visible period, (2 – 5 years), but the damage is still there. I do not recommend oats and rye for people who are sensitive to gluten. It is not really a hardship to do without these and a true gluten-free diet is 100 percent gluten-free.

There is controversy that some patients can tolerate oats or barley but a small bowel biopsy must be done first to obtain definite results.

HOSPITALISATION

Here are some tips to make a hospital stay safely manageable for someone on a gluten-free diet:

Before you leave home type out a clear list of exactly what it is you cannot tolerate. So often, people think we have said 'glucose' instead of 'gluten-free', or the person taking down your details may not speak English well enough and this way they can copy exactly what you have written. In my case, I am lactose intolerant and must also have a gluten-free and soya-free diet.

Take all your own regular medication with you and also list these before you leave home. This ensures that you are not dependant on medication which has not been thoroughly checked by your own pharmacist.

Do Not Take Anything for Granted.

The hospital will accommodate you in any way possible as long as they are clearly informed.

On arrival, call the ward sister and explain your problem. Request an introduction to the dietician and discuss all your needs very carefully. Decide on menus and check each meal before eating.

Take a little packet of rice cakes with you to snack on for when you begin to feel better, as the coffee shop will probably only be able to supply you with potato crisps.

If you will be staying longer than a day or two, make some melba toast to take with you so that you do not crave carbohydrates when you might be needing them most.

Don't be embarrassed to take responsibility for your needs, you deserve your good health.

Melba Toast

Slice gluten-free bread very thinly. Place on baking tray and spread with little herbed Cardin or Olé margarine. Bake for an hour at 95°C and then switch off and leave in oven overnight. Store in an airtight tin to keep crisp.

Tips for Travellers

AIR TRAVEL

The best procedure to follow is to request a gluten-free meal when you make your reservation and have it entered into the computer. However, this is not enough as the airlines continue, at this stage, to confuse 'vegetarian' with 'wheat-free'. It is best to state exactly what you want to eat.

If you are on an extended international flight, always take along your own emergency snack. Call the PRO of the airline 48 hours before departure to discuss your special request. If they see gluten-free requests often enough, they will become familiar with the dietary requirements. Watch the nuts – they may be rolled in flour.

Your gluten-free meal will be marked underneath your meal container. Check that you have the correct meal. At this point I am still working on the airlines so do not assume that any roll or biscuit supplied is gluten-free and do not eat anything that is unlabelled.

Take a menu to suit your requirements to the travel agency when you book or fax it direct to the airline ahead of your departure date. Here is an example of a menu:

Breakfast	Fresh fruit and / or juice Egg (not omelette, as this might contain a filling or flour) Grilled or baked mushrooms (without sauce) Grilled steak or haddock Rice cake and honey
Lunch and dinner	Smoked fish starter Grilled fish or meat (no sauce) Rice or potato Vegetable (no sauce) Salad (no dressing – unless labelled) Fruit salad Cheese Rice cakes

Bon Voyage

Catering for Your Gluten-free Guest

This is our hand-out for Granny, favourite aunt and your best friend's kitchen!

Please don't go to any trouble. We have tried to list the everyday foods you would normally have on your shelf. Please pin this in up your kitchen so that you can enjoy our visit as much as we enjoy visiting you.

YES WE DO EAT!

Meat	Grilled or roasted, no sauces Only Kosher sausages and polony (as they contain no filler)
Fish	Fried in maize meal or Kelloggs crumbs
Eggs	Yes
Fruit	Yes
Rice	Yes
Vegetables	Fresh, frozen or dehydrated Tinned – Koo tinned peas or brown beans Creamed sweetcorn
Other	IXL tomato sauce Worcester sauce Simba mayonnaise Mrs Ball's Chutney

Ready made foods that can be included:
Rice cakes, ice cream (no cones or wafers), yoghurt, cheese, drinking chocolate, Maizena, biltong, mebos, meringues and macaroons, nougat, only plain or salt and vinegar chips, nuts, raisins, dried fruits, Moirs instant pudding, Moirs crême caramel, Royal instant pudding, Kelloggs corn flakes, Rice Crispies, chocolates (except those containing wafers), popcorn, Nescafé pure coffee, Melrose pickles, tuna, asparagus, bean curd, Liquifruit, wine and rum, sesame seeds, sunflower seeds and natural licorice (available from health stores).

WE ARE NOT PERMITTED:

Mustard (watch salad dressings), spaghetti, noodles, instant soups, sauces, soya sauce, all flavours of crisps with the exception of plain and salt and vinegar, breadcrumbs, beer and whisky, wheat flour in any form, millet or wheat germ, bread, cakes and biscuits.

We will bring our own baked foods to make life easier for you.

Family Holidays

In order for the 'cook and bottle-washer' to have as much benefit from the holiday as other members of the family, do as much planning and baking in advance as possible. Everyone's appetites always seem larger on holiday.

Before leaving, bake your own bread and slice it. Freeze it on arrival.

Take a generous supply of gluten-free rusks and biscuits, Vital health rice biscuits and chinese rice noodles.

If possible, take a supply of Kosher polonies and sausages with you as these may not be readily available at your destination. Freeze these on arrival.

Ascertain what shopping facilities are available in the area. If these are limited, also take your special brands of gluten-free tinned foods, mayonnaise, tomato sauce and soup cubes, as well as gluten-free flour for quick pancakes.

Last, but not least, take your *Gluten-Free Guide for Southern Africa,* by Carole Smollan.

Gluten-free is hassle free if you plan ahead!

Biscuit Dough

Make this dough before you leave. Roll into a sausage shape and freeze. Transport in a cooler bag to keep frozen. Thaw slightly, slice and bake on arrival.

1 cup rice flour
1 cup gluten-free flour
1 cup Maizena
½ cup castor sugar
4 tablespoons margarine (Olé and Cardin are lactose-free)
1 egg
1tsp Royal baking powder
¼ cup lemon juice
grated lemon rind

Mix all the ingredients together.
Roll out and bake at 180°C for 12-15 minutes.
Store in an airtight container to keep crisp.

RESTAURANT EATING

If you are intending to eat in a restaurant, inform the manager of your problem when you make your reservation, and again when you arrive at the restaurant.

If you have a favourite restaurant, make sure the restauranteur has read *The Gluten- Free Guide for South Africa*. Help spread understanding of coeliac disease and you will be helping yourself.

It is a good idea to stick to grills, vegetables and salads, as sauces and puddings are usually suspect.

HANDY HINTS FOR HAPPY CHILDREN

It is most important for all concerned mothers to read the medical overviews very well. The recipes contained in the book should help considerably to illustrate how to approach gluten-free cooking.

Helpful Hints

- In order to keep your children's lives normal, get them into the habit of preparing their own tuck-boxes whenever they go out. So often I have been caught coming home lates, with only sandwiches available to buy. Fill a container with their biscuits or buns. I always include enough for curious friends. Good friends always let me provide our own plate of eats at their tea parties.

- It is always a good idea to phone the mother of your child's friends when they are invited to eat there or sleep over. Either inform her of what your child can eat or offer to bring something. I find this a better option as people are often unaware of what gluten-free food really entails. One can bring food as similar as possible to the standard menu.

- When eating in a restaurant order roast or grilled food, avoiding sauces, gravies and casseroles. Eggs are a good choice. Always ask about omelettes or mashed potato as these are often thickened with wheat flour or powdered milk.

- Chips are the coeliac mother's saving grace. All children love chips and crisps and these are usually readily available. Packets of crisps must be checked, as certain flavours contain flour. READ YOUR LABELS or play safe by choosing plain crisps.

- All Kosher meat is gluten-free. There are Kosher butcheries as well as Kosher departments in most large supermarkets. The available selection of sausages, polonies and boerewors offers plenty to choose from, and suppliers in the larger towns are usually helpful with special requests. I usually deep-freeze 25kg in small packs and find this most convenient.

- Most pack instant soups contain flour and cannot be used. I find the dehydrated mixed vegetables very handly. You can store these in a tupperware container and use as many as you need to make a very tasty soup.

- Ultra Care for Kids is a relatively new product available from health stores and chemists. It is a high-quality nutritional supplement for children from 1 – 12 years of age. It has a rice protein base which is extremely useful for children with dairy, gluten or soya hypersensitivities. It is also a source of dairy-free calcium. The product is balanced with essential fatty acids to nutritionally support central nervous system development. Is also a nutritional aid for post-antibiotic use. (For further information see chapter on Specialist Suppliers.)

Gluten-free Play-dough

Children should generally not eat their playthings. However, in all likelihood your nursery school is using play-dough. Children have a nasty habit of putting everything in their mouths. If you have a young child at nursery school, provide the teacher with a batch made gluten-free and explain the problem.

Play-dough Recipe

Mix together 1 cup salt
½ cup warm water
food colouring

Enough gluten-free flour to make a workable dough.
Add to warm water, colouring and salt.
Roll out onto a floured board to cool.
Wrap in plastic bag to keep soft.

Gluten-free Birthday Parties

Gluten-free birthday parties can be as much fun as any regular party.

For younger children you can serve:
Sweets (Read labels very carefully)
Crisps (check label if flavoured crisps are used)
Nuts and raisins
Ice-cream in cups or dishes (no cones)
Ice-cream suckers
Jelly

Any of the recipes in the general baking section of this book.

For older children:
Kosher sausages/polonies
Crisps (check label if flavoured crisps are used)
Home-made hamburgers
Cucumbers (fresh or pickled)
Cheese dips
Baked apples
Fish fingers (fried in mealie meal)
Sosaties
Baked potatoes
Any of the recipes in the general baking section of this book

NB: Consult the lists in the 'What to Buy' chapter of this book.

School Tours

It is not necessary for your child to miss out on school outings or excursions. Simple forward planning will make the meal management on the trip easy for your coeliac child. I have found schools and clubs very helpful in supplying the names and addresses of the hostels or hotels to be visited.

Next, ascertain how many of the meals will be pre-packed lunches (probably sandwiches) and where these will be prepared.

Write a short note to the manager of the hotel or hostel and explain your difficulty. Give simple suggestions of foodstuffs your child CAN safely eat. This will allow the manager to have suitable food on hand without his having to try to work out what is or isn't gluten-free.

Here is an example of a short list to include:

	ALLOWED	NOT ALLOWED
Breakfast	Mealie meal porridge without sauce or gravy	Bread rolls
	Corn Flakes	Biscuits
	Rice Krispies	Bread crumbs
	Haddock	Oats
	Steak	Wheat products
	Bacon	
	Vegetables	
	Fresh fruit	
	Stewed/canned fruit	
	Cheese	
	Eggs (no flour)	
	Yoghurt	
	Cream	
Lunch and Dinner	Meats, fish (grilled, roasted) No gravy	Mayonnaise
	Eggs (no flour)	Tomato sauce
	Vegetables (no sauce)	Salad dressings
	Plain chips, rice, mealie rice	No polonies or sausages, except specified labels
	Oil and vinegar salad dressing	Soup made from cubes or packets
	Maizena	Stew with gravy thickened with flour
	Ice-cream	
	Jelly	
	Fruit – fresh/stewed/canned	
	Baked apples	
	Hinds custard	

Here is an example of the letter I used which worked very well, although there was still some dissension when my child got roast beef for the third night in a row while the others got stew!

The Catering Manager

My child Tanya is due to arrive at your hostel on 11th June with the school netball team. She is a coeliac sufferer and must have a specialised diet. She is forbidden to eat anything containing wheat or wheat products.

It is very important for her health to maintain this diet strictly and I would appreciate it very much if your staff could ensure an alternative meal should she be unable to eat the meal being served. I enclose a short list of the usual things she CAN eat for you to plan ahead.

My very grateful thanks.

Carole Smollan

Suggestions for Packed Lunches

These suggestions are useful for everyday lunch as well as school tours:

Peanuts
Raisins
Biltong
Grilled or roasted cold meat
Cucumbers
Carrots
Rice biscuits
Liga (gluten-free) biscuits (blue box)
Cheese portions
Sesame snaps
Cheese straws (check label)
Banana bread
Popcorn
Talagu Mealie Bread (tinned)
Fruit/dried fruit
Plain flavoured chips (crisps)
Vital health rice biscuits
Chocolate (Dairy Milk, Bourneville or Albany)

The Marvellous Mealie

As mealie (maize) meal is the staple diet of this country, it is unnecessary to go to the expense of using imported products and flours. As it is gluten-free and versatile, it deserves a special mention.

Maize originates from Central America where it was cultivated by Red Indian tribes around 1492. It was brought to Europe by Christopher Columbus and was later taken as far afield as Asia and North Africa. In 1658 a packet of seed arrived in South Africa. Today it is the country's most important agricultural crop, and is available at all supermarkets.

Mealie meal is produced as several different products. For lighter baking mixtures choose a fine mealie meal such as bakers cones. For a more crumbly mixture choose coarser sifted meal which is preground and packed as dried porridge.

Maize is available as:

Green maize (mealies), seeds for popcorn, dried maize, maize oil, samp, mealie rice, Corn Flakes, Maizena – cornflour and mealie bread (available tinned as well as fresh). These products are generally produced from the large green mealies, but yellow maize meal is also available – generally from health stores.

South African maize terms

Kabu maize	unbroken maize
Stywe pap	stiff maize porridge
Slap pap	thin maize porridge
Putu pap	crumbly porridge

International maize terminology

USA	cornmeal mush
Ireland	stirabout
Rumania	mamaliga
South America	tamales
Mexico	tortillas

South Africans love outdoor entertaining and a braai is part of the culture of the country thanks to the wonderfully clement weather. Stiff maize porridge and a tomato sauce are the traditional accompaniments to the meat and are becoming more popular even among visitors to the country.

Stywe Pap (Stiff maize porridge)

2 cups water
½ teaspoon salt
1 cup mealie meal
½ tablespoon butter (optional)

Bring water to boil.
Add salt and mealie meal.
Cover and boil for five minutes.
Use a wooden spoon and stir well.
Cover and steam for further 20 minutes.
Spoon into a serving dish and use an ice-cream scoop to serve.

Sauce

3 tomatoes
2 onions
2 tablespoons oil
2 tablespoons tomato sauce
2 tablespoons vinegar or lemon juice
1 tablespoon brown sugar

Brown onions in oil. Add skinned chopped tomatoes. Add other ingredients. Serve hot with the pap and meat.

Zulu Putu (with thanks Caroline Kgaladi)

2 cups mealie meal
1 cup water
salt

Cook mealie meal with water until dry and crumbly.
Can be served as a fabulous dessert with canned peaches, lemon curd, or chocolate sauce.

What is Mealie Rice?

Mealie rice is a germless product manufactured from the endosperm of the maize kernel. It consists primarily of starch with a maximum fat content of 1.5% and a fibre content not exceeding 0.8%. Mealie rice is, therefore, a starch food. It can be served with foods such as vegetables, fruit and/or a protein food for nutritious and economical dishes.

Like its sister mealie meal, mealie rice is versatile, filling and inexpensive. Use it as you would use ordinary rice.

PREPARATION

Mealie rice need not necessarily be soaked, but soaking shortens the cooking time.

Overnight soaking process
Cover the mealie rice with sufficient water and soak overnight.

Rapid soaking process
Cover the mealie rice with water. Bring to the boil and cook for 10 minutes.
Turn heat off and leave to soak for an hour.

COOKING METHODS

Conventional method
Drain the soaked mealie rice in a colander or sieve. Rinse under cold running water to remove the excess starch. Cover with boiling water and cook until soft. Stir frequently with a fork. If the water boils away, add more boiling water. Drain the cooked rice and again rinse under cold running water.

Pressure cooking
Cover the mealie rice with boiling water and cook in the pressure cooker for 20 – 25 minutes at 200kP. Drain and rinse thoroughly.

Microwave method
Prepare the mealie rice as indicated. Add the rice to boiling water and microwave for 11 minutes on high (100%). Stir occasionally with a fork. Drain and rinse thoroughly.

STORAGE OF MEALIE RICE

Uncooked product
Uncooked mealie rice must be stored in an airtight container in a cool place. If it is to be stored for a long period you would be advised to keep it in the refrigerator or deep-freeze. Insect infestation is thus avoided.

Cooked product
Cooked mealie rice can be stored for 2 – 3 days in an airtight container in the refrigerator.

FREEZING

Cooked rice can also be stored in the deep-freeze. Store in plastic bags or containers for not longer than three months. The texture of the maize rice will change and it will become floury if it is stored for longer than three months. Drain the maize rice thoroughly to avoid freezer burn. It is useful to freeze in portions so that you do not need to defrost more than is required.

DEFROSTING

Conventional method
Leave the rice to defrost overnight in the refrigerator or leave the rice for 5 – 6 hours at room temperature to defrost naturally.

Microwave method
Put the mealie rice in the microwave for five minutes at medium (50%) for every 350g (500ml) of rice. Stir the rice once during the defrosting process.

See recipe section for Steamed Mealie Bread and Mealie Shortcake.

What to Buy – Gluten-free Foods

Health Food Shops that Stock Gluten-free Foods

(This is not a comprehensive list of health stores. It is just a few stores that definitely stock gluten-free products.)

Bloemfontein

Bon Vita

Cape Town

Good Stuff
Nature's Best

Durban

Healthy Life

Gauteng

Balfour Park Health Shop
Fruits and Roots (Yeoville)
Health & Thyme (Randburg)
Health Seekers (Norwood)
Health & Homeopathic Products (Heathway Centre, Blackheath)
Healthworks (Hyde Park)
Mary Ann's Wholefood Emporium (Craighall)
Natural Health (Fourways Mall)
Natural Remedies (Westgate)
Naturally Healthy (South)
Perfect Health (Midrand)
Reform Haus (Bryanston)
Reform Haus (Gallo Manor)
Sandton Health & Herb (Sandton)

Knysna

Lesley's Health Shop

Pretoria

Arcadia Health (Arcadia Centre)
Continental Herbs (Esselen Street)
Gwen's Health (Sanlam Centre)
Health Oasis (Pretoria)

Somerset West

Nature's Den

For most of us, chocolate is an essential to life. On a gluten-free diet be wary of eating chocolate sauce in a restaurant unless you are allowed to check the label on the bottle yourself. For coeliacs with the added limitation of lactose intolerance, remember to use only Nestlé cocoa powder or Nestlé Nesquik chocolate, as Cadburys Bourneville, or Nestlé Hot Chocolate contain milk. The Nestlé list of acceptable sweets and chocolates gives plenty of choice.

Nestlé consumer queries (011) 889 6116

NESTLÉ PRODUCTS

NESTLÉ CHOCOLATES

Albany	Gluten-free
Coconut Crunch	Gluten-free
Crême de Café	Gluten-free
Dolce Fruit	Gluten-free
Dolce Milk	Gluten-free
Dolce Nut	Gluten-free
Easy-Melt Dark Coating	Gluten-free
Easy-Melt Milk Coating	Gluten-free
Easy-Melt White Coating	Gluten-free
Fruit and Nut	Gluten-free
Full Cream Milk Chocolate	Gluten-free
Milk Chocolate Assortment	Gluten-free
Milky Bar	Gluten-free
Milky Bar Crackle	Gluten-free
Mint Crunch	Gluten-free
Peppermint Creams	Gluten-free
Sucrose Free Dark Chocolate	Gluten-free
Sucrose Free Milk Chocolate	Gluten-free
Sucrose Free Milk Chocolate with Fruit & Nuts	Gluten-free
Sucrose Free Milk Chocolate with Toasted Rice	Gluten-free
Sucrose Free White Chocolate	Gluten-free

Super Almonds	Gluten-free
Super Hazels	Gluten-free
Thin Peppermints	Gluten-free
Thoughts	Gluten-free
Whole Nut	Gluten-free
Nestlé Morsels	Gluten- and lactose-free

INSTANT DRINKS

Cocoa	Gluten- and lactose-free
Encore	Gluten- and lactose-free
Hot Chocolate	Gluten-free
Nescafé Classic	Gluten- and lactose-free
Nescafé Espresso	Gluten- and lactose-free
Nescafé Finesse	Gluten- and lactose-free
Nescafé Gold	Gluten- and lactose-free
Nescafé Select	Gluten- and lactose-free
Nesquik Chocolate	Gluten- and lactose-free
Nesquik Cream Soda	Gluten- and lactose-free
Nesquik Strawberry	Gluten- and lactose-free
Ricoffy Caffeine Free	Gluten- and lactose-free
Ricoffy Regular	Gluten- and lactose-free
Carnation Milk Products	Gluten-free
Ideal Coffee Cream	Gluten-free

NESTLÉ CEREALS

Nestum Rice and Maize	Gluten- and lactose-free

NESTLÉ FOOD SERVICE EXCLUSIVES

C & B Fruit Chutney	Gluten- and lactose-free
C & B Tomato Sauce	Gluten- and lactose-free
Crême Caramel Powder	Gluten- and lactose-free
Crême Caramel Sauce	Gluten- and lactose-free
Maggi Aspic Jelly	Gluten- and lactose-free
Maggi Basic Sauce – Brown	Gluten- and lactose-free
Maggi Instant Stock Powder	Gluten- and lactose-free
Maggi Mash	Gluten-free
Maggi Rich Gravy Mix	Lactose-free
Nestlé Caramel Flavoured Coating Chocolate	Gluten- and lactose-free
Nestlé Chocolate Sauce	Gluten- and lactose-free

Nestlé Dessert	
– Chocolate, Caramel & Strawberry Mousse	Gluten-free
Nestlé Dessert	
– Strawberry / Peach / Apricot	Gluten-free
Nestlé Dessert Topping	Gluten- and lactose-free
Nestum No 1 Rice and Maize	Gluten- and lactose-free
AL 110	Gluten- and lactose-free
Alfare	Gluten- and lactose-free
Lactogen No 1	Gluten-free
Lactogen No 2	Gluten-free

Maggi Products

Brown onion soup	Gluten- and lactose-free
Chicken and mushroom slim soup	Gluten- and lactose-free
Fondor	Gluten- and lactose-free
Fondor – chilli	Gluten- and lactose-free
Lazenby Worcester Sauce	Gluten- and lactose-free
Maggi seasoning	Gluten- and lactose-free
Mongolian Stir-fry Mix	Gluten- and lactose -ree
Napoli Pasta Sauce Mix	Gluten- and lactose-free
Oriental Stir-fry Mix	Gluten- and lactose-free
Satay Beef Stir-fry Mix	Gluten- and lactose-free
Soup- spring vegetable	Gluten- and lactose-free
Stock	
– Instant chicken powder	Gluten- and lactose-free
– Chicken tablet	Gluten- and lactose-free
– Chicken tablets (Extra)	Gluten- and lactose-free
– Instant beef powder	Gluten- and lactose-free
– Beef tablets	Gluten- and lactose-free
– Beef tablets (Extra)	Gluten- and lactose-free
Sweet and Sour Stir-fry Mix	Gluten- and lactose-free

Crosse & Blackwell Products

Chilli Mayonnaise	Gluten- and lactose-free
Chilli Relish	Gluten- and lactose-free
Chilli Sauce	Gluten- and lactose-free
Custard Powder	Gluten- and lactose-free
Mayonnaise	Gluten- and lactose-free
Salad Cream	Gluten- and lactose-free
Sandwich Spread	Gluten- and lactose-free
Tomato Relish	Gluten- and lactose-free
Trim Low Oil Dressing	Gluten- and lactose-free

Moirs Products

Moirs produce a very comprehensive list indicating which products are gluten-free, lactose-free and soya-free. These are very useful in making your baking more interesting.

Consumer queries (011) 454-2866

The following products are gluten-free:

Moirs instant puddings are gluten-free and can be made with Rice Dream or Orley Whip if they need to be lactose-free. Flavours that are permitted are:
butterscotch, caramel, chocolate, strawberry, vanilla.

Chocolate chips (NB: vermicilli contains lactose)
Hundreds and thousands
Moirs baking powder
Moirs coconut
Moirs colourings
Moirs Crême Caramel
Moirs custard powder
Moirs essences
Moirs Meat Magic
Moirs silver balls
Moirs spices and seasoning in barbeque, oriental, mexican and sosatie flavours

Hulley and Rice Products

These products are gluten-free
Baking powder
Chilli powder
Masala mix
Turmeric

Cadbury's Products

These are gluten-free but contain lactose
Bourneville Cocoa Powder
Cadbury's Hot Chocolate
Cadbury's Milk Mates
Cadbury's Smash

Ina Paarman Products

These products are gluten-free

Salad Dressings
Mustard
Herb
Garlic
Lite Salad Splash
Italian Lite
Salad Splash
French Lite Salad Splash

Basting sauces
Lemon and herb
Peri-peri
Spicy curry
Sun dried tomato
Apple and soy
Mossies mustard
Mossies green peppercorn

KEY HEALTH PRODUCTS

Manufacturers of gluten- and lactose-free carob products:

Carob coated rice cakes
Yoghurt covered rice cakes

Carob chocolate mini bars in the following flavours:
peanut and raisin
muesli sesame and sunflower
peanut
coconut
plain carob

Gluten-free pasta is a new and very welcome product on the South African market. Do not purchase any product that does not list the ingredients. These products cook more quickly than ordinary pasta and need to be watched carefully.

To Cook A Perfect Italian Pasta

(By courtesy of David Alessio Merlini)

Fill a saucepan with 5 litres of water for 500g of pasta.
Boil water, add salt.
When water boils again add the pasta and cook for 6 minutes.
To test if the pasta is ready, select a piece, bite it, and if it is still white in the centre the pasta is not ready to eat.
Pour all the water off immediately, and pour 1 tablespoon of oil over the pasta.

La Pasta Delizia (011) 786-6767

They produce gluten-free, lactose-free fettucini, lasagne and spaghetti. They prepare gluten-free take-away spaghetti bolognaise which is also available to be ordered by clinics and hospitals who need to cater for patients on gluten-free diets. They also manufacture pumpkin gnocci, beetroot macaroni, vegetable fettucini and carrot fettucini which is gluten-free, lactose-free and soya-free.

Southbakels produce a gluten-free flour suitable for making pasta for those that have a pasta maker at home.

Pasta Regalo in Cape Town produce gluten-free fettucini, spaghetti, macaroni and lasagne.

Pasta Marco in Pretoria, (012) 804-3426 Fax (012) 804-1407, product gluten-free fettucini.

Chinese rice noodles are wonderful for thickening soup or casseroles and are available at most stores.

Polony King Products

The following products are gluten-free:

Brawn plain
Curry brawn
Chicken in aspic
Turkey breast
Baked ham loaf
Berliner Zungenwurst
Bierschinken
Bierwurst loaf
Blutspeckwurst ring
Edelweiss
Fleischwurst
Hollandse Rookwors
Mushroom loaf
Paprika Lyoner
Pepper loaf
Cooked silverside
Pastrami loaf
Pressed tongue
Breaola cabanossi
Parma ham
Westphalian ham
Prosciutto Cotto
Kassler rib (cooked)
Kassler roll
Lachsschinken
Bacon and egg loaf
Olive loaf
Pimento loaf
Cheese Griller cocktail sausages
Salames Brotform pfeffer salami
Cervelate
Cooked salami
Hungarian salami
Italian salami
Pepperoni
Salami
Milano

Sausages
Bockwurst
Cheese griller
Frankfurter
German Viennas
Weisswurst
Jagdwurst
Krakauer
Country sausage
Schinkenwurst

Paola Classy Snacks

Manufacturers of:
Gluten-free bread
Gluten-free fruit bread
Amaretto
Gian Duia
Coconut macaroons
Nut Fantasy
Coffee Nut
Rice Snaps
They will also bake to order a selection of egg-free and dairy-free biscuits.

Mrs Bread Cares

Manufacturers of:
Gluten-free bread
Soya bread
Polenta bread
Carob and corn muffins
Gluten-free cakes baked to order

Pouyoukas Health Foods

A gluten-free diet excludes many of the fibre foods. One must not only be conscious of eliminating those that contain gluten, but make a concerted effort to replace the products with fibre that is gluten-free. Pouyoukas Foods market a wide range of products suitable for replacing foods containing Vitamin B, such as sesame seeds, sunflower seeds, poppy seeds, nuts, raisins, chickpeas, wild rice and many more. They also manufacture a range of gluten-free flours which will make your baking more varied and in this way add many different minerals and vitamins to the diet,
eg Buckwheat flour, polenta, rice flour, potato flour and yellow mealie meal.

Super 'A' Norwood

Stocks a wide range of gluten-free foods.

At this store you will find:

- Classy Snax gluten-free bread
- Gluten-free biscuits
- Hoummous
- Ina Paarman sauces
- Indonesian rice noodles
- Indonesian soy sauce
- Kosher sausages and polonies
- Lemon sauce
- Meringues
- Osem soups
- Oyster sauce
- Poppadoms
- Pouyoukas flours
- Rice cakes
- Tahina
- Telma soups
- Tofu

Rice Dream

Made from organically grown brown rice, this is the gourmet answer to replacing milk products in your recipes.

Rice is one of the least allergenic foods and is easy to digest and enjoy, providing much needed energy, calcium, vitamins A and D.

It can be used to thicken casseroles, make a creamy sauce, or poach fish. To give my family extra nutrition, I use Rice Dream in jellies, puddings and mousse, or as a substitute where recipes call for milk products.

Parev and Kosher.

For a free recipe book please call (011) 616-7074.

Take-away Foods

Be very careful when eating take-away food. Many take-out recipes contain gluten and should be checked with the manager before purchasing.

Nandos Chicken

Sauces and marinades are all gluten-free and lactose-free. This is a real plus for quick meals.

Steers

All sauces contain gluten and are NOT ALLOWED.

Royco Products

The following products are gluten-free:
Royco Lite Chutney (contains lactose) Mild and Hot
Royco Cup A Soup (contains lactose) Hearty Beef
Royco Lite Salad Dressing in the following flavours:
Italian
Creamy French
1000 Island
French

Also gluten-free:
Mrs Ball's Chutney – Peach, Hot and Mild
Fray Bentos Spread

Quick Reference List of Gluten-free Products Used in the Recipes in this Book

Apple cider
Asparagus
Beans, peas, chickpeas
Bicarbonate of soda
Bovril
Butter
Caraway seeds
Cardin oil
Castor sugar
Coconut
Coleman's mustard
Cottage cheese
Fresh herbs
Fruit squash
Gelatin
Golden syrup
Ground almonds
Honey
Hoummous
Icing sugar
Ina Paarman's basting sauce
Ina Paarman's salad dressings
Jelly
Kayo food enhancer
Key Health carob cakes
Knorr Aromat
Koo Sweetcorn
Lawry's Tacos
Lazenby's Worcester Sauce
Liga Gluten-ex biscuits
Liquifruit
Maizena
Maple syrup
Marmite
Mealie meal
Mebos
Mrs Breadcare
Nestlé (see separate list)
Nestlé cocoa
Nougat
Nuts
Olé margarine
Olive oil
Orley Whip
Peanut butter
Pecan nuts
Polenta
Popcorn
Poppadoms
Poppy seed
Poupon mustard
Purity rice cereal
Raisins
Rice cakes (Vital, Key Health)
Rice Dream
Rice flour
Rice pudding
Rooibos tea
Robertson's cinnamon and nutmeg
Sesame seed
Sesame snaps
Sherry
Snoek flakes
Soya flour
Tahina
Talagu corn bread
Tartaric Acid
Telma, Osem chicken soup
Telma potato latkes
Trim seafood dressing
Water chestnuts

Do's and Don'ts of Gluten-free Baking

People who have just been informed of their medical need for a gluten-free diet call me in horror, imagining that they can never again eat the good things in life.

A lot of substitution is required to alter regular recipes for a completely gluten-free diet. However, once you become familiar with the products available you will feel more confident to experiment on your own. You need only look at the photograph on the front cover of this book to see that many delicious foods are within your reach. It is well worth the trouble of learning the new techniques of baking and cooking to be able to live a happy, healthy and also delicious lifestyle.

Don't get discouraged if your gluten-free bread and cakes come out looking flat and unappetising at first, you will improve with practise.

It is absolutely essential to replace gluten carbohydrates and find alternative sources of starch and fibre. A well balanced diet with all the nutrients you need is the secret of managing a gluten-free diet well.

It works well to mix a selection of gluten-free flours into your recipe, as this provides a variety of nutritional values.

Rice flour or potato flour work best when mixed together, as the rice flour is quite rough while the potato flour is smooth. Together the consistency is much improved. Potato flour is sometimes in short supply but can be substituted with mashed potato combined with another flour.

To make potato starch which is an excellent binding agent:

Grate the potatoes on a large stringy grater and drain through a muslin bag for a few hours. Let the strained juice stand for a few hours and then pour the liquid off. The remaining pulp is the potato starch which can be added to other gluten-free flours as a binder.

Mealie meal and soya flour are better when mixed with another flour.

When converting a wheat flour recipe to gluten-free flour, use a little more baking powder than originally stated.

GLUTEN-FREE BAKING POWDER

85g cornflour
85g bicarbonate of soda
75g cream of tartar
75g tartaric acid

Mix all ingredients together. Pass through a fine sieve two or three times. Store in an airtight bottle in a dry place.

APPROXIMATE SUBSTITUTES WHEN CONVERTING FROM WHEAT FLOUR TO GLUTEN-FREE FLOUR

Use any one of the following substitutes to replace 1 cup of wheat flour:
1 cup gluten-free flour
¾ cup potato flour
¾ cup rice flour
1 cup Maizena
1 scant cup fine mealie meal
¾ cup coarse mealie meal
Soya flour is best mixed with the other flours.

Green Oasis produce a range of baking mixes which are gluten-free:
Buckwheat Crumpets
Corn Waffles
Corn Bread Mix
Corn Pizza

- Do not try to get the consistency of your batter for baking cakes and breads looking like ordinary flour batter. It should usually be lighter and slightly thinner like yoghurt.

- When flouring your board or baking tins, use Maizena rather than gluten-free flour. It tastes better.

- I have found that gluten-free flour bakes best in baking foil and works well in the microwave.

It is always safest and best to eat simple whole foods with no hidden additives and ingredients – fresh meat, fish, salads and vegetables, 100% pure fruit drinks and to ensure that all your medication is checked as being gluten-free.

As you get to know which ingredients and products are safe for you, you can broaden your shopping list until everything on your shelf at home is safe to use in your cooking and baking.

Never rely on any storekeeper who sells a product that does not carry an ingredients label. Contact the manufacturer direct and take responsibility for your own wellbeing.

List of Ingredients to Enhance your Baking and Cooking which you ARE ALLOWED on a Gluten-free Diet

Agar-Agar
A vegetarian binding agent.

Buckwheat
A starchy seed belonging to the rhubarb family. Sometimes mixed with wheat, so do check labels very carefully. Used to make noodles and cereal.

Caraway
A dried seed derived from a plant belonging to the parsley family.

Carob
A bean of the carob tree originating from South America, ground and used as an excellent substitute for chocolate. Pleasant flavour and good brown colour.

Cocoa
A roasted bean from the cacao tree.

Corn Flakes
Manufactured from samp and marketed as cereal.

Cumin
A plant from the Mediterranean, usually used in powdered form.

Corn Flour
Maize flour and cornflour are often confused. Cornflour is a commercial maize starch, produced by a wet milling process. Generally sold under the trade name Maizena or Maizecor. Cornflour is similar to custard powder without the flavouring and is used for thickening sauces or setting a pudding, whereas maize flour is the milled maize used as a flour for baking.

Dahl (Dal) – Red Lentils
Used in Indian curries and casseroles.

Gelatin
A protein used as a binding agent to thicken or set your pudding. Not suitable for vegetarians as it is derived from the hooves of animals.

Gram Flour
Made from chickpeas. Has a lovely nutty flavour. Available from the Oriental Plaza or specialised health stores. Also known as Besan.

Guar gum
A texture modifying agent which will give your bread the elasticity that it lacks without gluten.

Hoummous
Also made from chickpeas.

Kelp
From seaweed.

Lecithin
A pleasant-tasting spread which can be used to substitute butter or fat.

Mustard seeds
Coleman's and Dijon.

Psyllium
A seed from the plantain family, often used in laxative products or for dietary bulking.

Sago
Derived from the palm tree. Used in puddings.

Sorghum
From corn.

Tapioca
Made from cassava. Used as a thickening agent in cakes and puddings

Tofu
Bean curd made from soya milk.

Urd
An Indian bean used in curries and puddings.

Xanthum gum
Made by fermenting glucose. Used to make the texture of baking lighter.

Products that Contain Hidden Gluten and are NOT PERMITTED on a Gluten-free Diet

Burgar-Burghul (cracked wheat – usually found in wheat salad)
Chips or potato skins at restaurants
Crisps (some flavours are not permitted)
Durum wheat
Farina
Gluten flour
Graham flour
Hydrolised vegetable protein (HVP) (ingredients must be checked)
Instant coffee (may contain barley)
Malt vinegar
Matzo meal
Mayonnaise
Modified food starch (could contain wheat, semolina or corn)
Mustard
Oat bran
Roasted nuts (may be rolled in flour)
Soya sauce
Spaghetti sauces
Spelt-dinkel
Spices
Syrups (made from a barley base)
Tomato sauce
Triticate (cross between wheat and rye)
Wheat germ

General Baking

CAKES

BRENDA'S CHOCOLATE CAKE

4 eggs
250ml sugar
45ml cocoa
125ml boiling water
125ml oil
5ml vanilla
375g gluten-free flour
3 teaspoons baking powder

Preheat oven to 180°C.
Grease two small baking tins.
Beat eggs and sugar until creamy.
Mix cocoa and boiling water in a cup then add to mixture, followed by the oil and vanilla.
Fold in dry ingredients. Pour into tins and bake for 30 mins.
Cool and then sandwich together with strawberry jam. Ice with chocolate icing.

Chocolate icing
2 tablespoons margarine
2 cups icing sugar
3 tablespoons cocoa
3 tablespoons Nesquick
3 tablespoons lemon juice
Mix well. Must be fairly stiff. Ice cake when cool.

MAIZE BOSTON BREAD

1 cup maize (mealie) meal
1 cup potato flour
½ cup rice bran (gluten-free)
1 cup golden syrup
2 eggs
2 teaspoons bicarbonate of soda
2 teaspoons Cardin margarine
1 cup diet Coke

Melt Cardin with syrup and butter.
Add Coke.
Mix with dry ingredients and eggs and bake for one hour at 180°C.

SHORTCAKE

¾ cup castor sugar
3 eggs
1¾ cups of gluten-free flour
1 heaped teaspoon butter
½ cup boiling water
2 teaspoons baking powder
pinch salt
1 teaspoon vanilla essence

Beat the sugar and eggs to a thick cream.
Fold in the flour and then the butter which has been melted in the boiling water.
Fold in vanilla and baking powder.
Bake at 200°C for 12 minutes in two 23cm tins.
Spread a layer of whipped cream between the cakes and garnish with strawberries or jam etc.

GLUTEN-FREE CARROT CAKE

275g gluten-free flour
60g Moirs baking powder
30g cinnamon
pinch salt
30g nutmeg
150g brown sugar
175ml sunflower oil
90g pecan nuts
150g coarsely grated carrots
½ tin crushed pineapple or 2 mashed bananas

Mix dry ingredients, add eggs and then add the oil and carrots.
Bake for 45 mins at 180°C.
This is a soft moist cake.
For a cream cheese topping sweeten a carton of cream cheese and use in the same way as butter icing.

For those of you who are lactose intolerant omit the cream cheese and substitute:
1 sachet Orley Whip
200g icing sugar
Dash of lemon juice
Top with sugared almonds

The problem with this cake is that the family devour it immediately!

BUTTERSCOTCH CAKE

4 eggs
1 cup sugar
1 pkt Moirs butterscotch pudding
½ cup boiling water
3 tablespoons oil
1½ cups gluten-free flour
3 teaspoons Moirs baking powder

Grease two smallish baking tins.
Beat eggs and sugar till creamy.
Add pudding powder, oil and boiling water and mix well.
Fold in dry ingredients.
Bake for 30 mins.
Cool and sandwich together with some of the icing mix.

Serve warm as a winter dessert with Butterscotch Schnapps

Topping
1 cup icing sugar
1 pkt Moirs butterscotch pudding
Water

Mix together until smooth and creamy and use as icing.

BANANA BREAD (Freezes well)

1¾ cups gluten-free flour
2 teaspoons gluten-free baking powder
¼ teaspoon bicarbonate of soda
½ teaspoon salt
2 tablespoons butter
¾ cup sugar
2 eggs
1 cup mashed ripe bananas
½ cup chopped pecan nuts

Sift flour, baking powder, bicarb and salt together.
Cream butter and sugar.
Add eggs one at a time and beat till light and fluffy and add to flour mixture.
Add mashed banana and nuts.
Blend well.
Bake in loaf pan on grease proof paper at 175°C for approximately 1 hour.

GLUTEN-FREE SPONGE CAKE

4 eggs
150g castor sugar
1 teaspoon vanilla essence
60g gluten-free flour
60g Maizena

Preheat oven to 180°C.
Separate eggs.
Whisk yolks with sugar and essence for at least 30 seconds until creamy.
Add flour and fold in with spatula.
Whisk egg whites until stiff and add to mixture.
Line tin with foil and bake for 50 minutes until 'springy'.

GINGERBREAD

250g maize meal
2 teaspoons Moirs baking powder
¼ teaspoon bicarbonate of soda
2 teaspoons cinnamon
2 tablespoons custard powder
125g castor sugar
10 tablespoons golden syrup
1 egg
1 pkt Orley Whip or 250g fresh cream

Cream butter and sugar together.
Beat in egg and golden syrup.
Mix in flours and bake for 50 minutes at 180°C.
Remove and cool.
Sprinkle with castor sugar.

GORGEOUS CRUNCHY APPLE TART

Short Crust
½ cup melted butter
1½ cups gluten-free flour
2 teaspoons gluten-free baking powder
1 tablespoon castor sugar
pinch salt
1 - 2 tablespoons apricot jam

Melt butter and add the sifted dry ingredients.
Combine to make smooth dough and line pie plate.
Spread thin layer of apricot jam.

Filling
7 - 8 apples, peeled, cored and sliced
pinch salt
½ cup sugar
2 tablespoons water
1 tablespoon currants

Cook apples with water and sugar until tender.
Mix with currants and spoon onto the prepared crust.

Crunchy Topping
4 tablespoons butter
¾ cup castor sugar
2 egg yolks
1 cup corn flakes

Cream butter and sugar.
Mix in egg yolks and beat well.
Gently stir in corn flakes.
Top the apple tart and bake in preheated over at 230°C for 30 minutes.

EASY CHRISTMAS CAKE

½ kg dried mixed fruit
½ cup cherries
1 cup nuts
1 teaspoon cinnamon
1 teaspoon ginger
1 cup brown sugar
3 tablespoons butter
1 cup hot water
1 cup mealie meal
1 cup gluten-free flour
1 teaspoon bicarbonate of soda
1 egg

Boil together fruit, sugar, butter and water for 5 minutes.
Allow to cool.
Add rest of ingredients and mix well.
Line a large cake tin with paper, allowing 2cm of paper above the tin.
Bake at 175°C for 1½ hours.

CHEESECAKE DE LUXE

Crumb Base
250g Kellogg's corn flake crumbs
3 tablespoons margarine
1 teaspoon ginger powder

Melt margarine, add ginger.
Remove from stove.
Add crumbs and stir well.
Pat into oiled dish and add cheese mixture.

Cheese Mixture
¾ cup sugar
½ kg cream cheese
1 tablespoon gluten-free flour
salt
6 eggs (separated)
1 cup thick cream
juice and rind of 1 lemon

Beat egg whites till stiff.
Mix all ingredients together.
Pour into base and bake at 180°C for ±1 hour until set.
Cool and serve with fruit.

FAIRYLIGHT CHOCOLATE CAKE

1 cup sugar
1½ cups gluten-free flour
4 eggs
¼ cup oil
¾ cup cocoa dissolved in ½ cup boiling water
salt
2½ teaspoons gluten-free baking powder

Sift sugar and flour togeter.
Make well in the centre and add the unbeaten eggs, one at a time.
Add the oil and cocoa. Beat well.
Add baking powder and stir in gently.
Fold in stiffly beaten egg whites.
Bake in large tins at 190°C for 20-25 minutes.

SNOW TOPPING FOR PLAIN CAKES

75ml margarine
250ml sunflower oil
1 teaspoon vanilla essence
90ml cream
50g sugar

Bring to the boil.
Allow to cool and ice cake with mixture.

FREEZER CHEESE CAKE

1 small can crushed pineapple
2 tubs cottage cheese
¾ cup sugar
1 egg
1 teaspoon vanilla essence
1 cup Kellogg's corn flake crumbs
butter

Melt butter, combine with crumbs, allow to cool.
Mix other ingredients well and line loaf pan with foil.
Place alternate layers of crumbs and thick cheese mixture in the loaf pan until full.
Freeze and then remove from pan and ice with thin chocolate icing. Keep frozen.
Remove ten minutes before eating and slice required amount.
Return the rest to freezer.

PASTRY

QUICK TART BASE

2 cups Kellogg's crumbs
1 cup melted butter
3 tablespoons sugar
Melt butter, add sugar and crumbs.
Stir well and pour into greased pie dish.
Allow to cool.

Suggestions for fillings
Custard
Cheese
Tinned fruits
Apples or seasonal fruits
Instant pudding (See 'What to Buy' chapter for permitted flavours.)

PIE PASTRY

170g gluten-free flour
85g butter or margarine
2 eggs
pinch of salt

Cream the fat, add the beaten eggs and gluten-free flour.
Roll to approx 5mm thick.
Bake at 220°C until brown.
Enough for a 23cm pie.

INSTANT POTATO PIE

1 packet instant potato (Maggi or Cadbury)
2 tablespoons gluten-free flour or potato flour
salt and pepper
60g butter
2 large onions
mushrooms
1 cup milk

Make potato as directed on packet.
Add 30g flour, salt and pepper and butter. Beat until smooth.
Place in oven-proof plate. Build up sides to hold filling.
Brown chopped onions in remaining butter.
Add mushrooms, 1 tablespoon flour and mix well.
Cook for 2 minutes.
Remove from heat and slowly add milk.
Return to stove and stir until thickened.
Pour into prepared flan and bake in medium oven for 25 minutes.

Alternatives to mushroom filling
Cheese
Flaked snoek
Tuna
Bacon
Asparagus

PASTRY FOR SAVOURIES

226g cream cheese
226g butter
226g gluten-free flour

Rub butter into flour and bind with cheese.
Knead into a smooth pastry and store in fridge to use when required.
Roll out thinly and cover with leftovers, mince, asparagus or cream cheese.
For a cheesy flavour, top with grated cheese, salt and pepper.
Bake in a hot oven for 10 minutes.
For sweeter biscuits add a tablespoon of sugar and glaze with beaten egg before baking. Roll in castor sugar when baked.

SAVOURY PASTRY FOR PIZZA

150g gluten-free flour
salt
60g margarine
Cayenne pepper
Soda water

Sift dry ingredients.
Add enough soda water to make a workable, rolling consistency dough.
Leave to cool.
Roll out thinly and cut into rounds.
Top with grated cheese, sliced tomato, anchovies etc. and bake at 220°C till golden and crisp.

INDIVIDUAL PIZZA

Potato pastry (recipe in this section)
Melrose cheese spread
Anchovies
Sliced tomatoes
Mushrooms

Half fill patty pans with potato pastry and cover with cheese spread, slices of tomato and top with anchovies and mushrooms. Bake for 30 minutes until edges leave the pan.
Serve hot with salad.

POTATO PASTRY

2 cups mashed potato
4 tablespoons butter
1 teaspoon baking powder
1 cup gluten-free flour

Add baking powder and salt to flour, then add the butter.
Add mashed potato and blend well.
Mix in enough warm water to make a stiff pastry that will roll out.
Bake in moderate oven approx 180°C for 40 minutes.

EGG AND BACON PIE

Add 2 scrambled eggs to the potato pastry, decorate with strips of half grilled bacon and return to oven for 20 minutes.

BISCUITS, BUNS AND COOKIES

GINGER BISCUITS

½ cup syrup
3 tablespoons oil
¾ cup sugar
2 eggs
1½ tablespoons ginger
1 teaspoon bicarbonate of soda, dissolved in ¼ cup boiling water
1 teaspoon each of cinnamon and mixed spice
gluten-free flour

Mix syrup, sugar and oil.
Add eggs, spice and bicarbonate of soda.
Add enough flour to make a soft dough.
Roll into balls. Flatten with a fork.
Bake in over at 375°C.

CRYSTAL COOKIES

Bake plain cookies
Topping: 1 pkt jelly
Mix 1 cup water into half a pkt jelly and coat the top of the cookie.
Then dip the cookie into dry jelly crystals coating the top in various colours.
Allow to dry.

RICE BISCUITS

226g rice flour
113g sugar
113g butter
2 eggs
Cream butter, add sugar and rice flour.
Beat eggs and then add slowly to mixture
Bake for 12 – 18 minutes at 180°C.

BANANA CRACKLE COOKIES

2 cups flour
½ teaspoon bicarbonate of soda
¾ teaspoon cinnamon
½ teaspoon salt
¾ cup margarine
3 tablespoons honey
1 egg
2 cups Rice Krispies
1 cup mashed bananas
1 cup chopped nuts

Sift flour, bicarb and salt together.
Cream margarine and sugar and add egg. Beat thoroughly.
Stir in bananas, nuts and lastly Rice Krispies.
Add dry ingredients.
Spoon dough onto baking tray about 5cm apart and bake for 15 minutes at 180°C.

NUT 'N HONEY LIGA BISCUITS

2 egg whites
1 cup chopped nuts
¾ cup honey
1 pkt Liga biscuits
Beat egg whites and honey well.
Place over a dish of hot water.
Beat for a further 7 minutes.
When icing retains shape, add nuts and then spread over biscuits.

CUSTARD BISCUITS

7 tablespoons gluten-free flour
3 tablespoons icing sugar
170g butter
85g custard powder (Hinds or Moirs allowed)
Mix ingredients together.
Roll out and cut into shapes.
Bake at 175°C until brown.

CORN FLAKE CRUNCHIES

1 cup gluten-free flour
1 cup sugar
1 cup crushed nuts
2 cups corn flakes
6 tablespoons butter
1 tablespoon syrup
1 teaspoon bicarbonate of soda

Melt butter and syrup.
Add bicarb and cool.
Add dry ingredients and pat into greased baking sheet.
Bake at 150°C until brown.
Cut into squares.

SOUTH AFRICAN SHORTBREAD

2 cups mealie meal
½ cup cornflour
pinch salt
95g castor sugar
2 teaspoons Moirs strawberry essence
220g butter

Sift dry ingredients together and rub in 220g butter.
Pat into biscuit tray, 5cm thick.
Prick with fork.
Bake in moderate over at 175°C for appoximately 20 minutes till creamy in colour.
Allow to cool before removing from pan.

SCOTCH SHORTBREAD

2 cups gluten-free flour
¼ cup cornflour
salt
113g castor sugar
220g butter

Same method as South African Shortbread.

MALLOW KRISPIES

28g margarine
2 cups Rice Krispies
1 pkt marshmallows

Melt margarine and marshmallows in a double boiler.
When smooth, add the Krispies and spoon into paper cookie cups.

ROCK-BUNS

½ cup mealie meal
½ cup cornflour
2 tablespoons skim-milk powder
4 tablespoons butter
1 egg (beaten)
2 tablespoons water
2 teaspoons gluten-free baking powder
1 cup raisins
1 tablespoon sugar

Mix dry ingredients together.
Add butter, eggs and water. Mix well and add raisins.
Bake in greased muffin pans at 245°C for 10 to 20 minutes.
Sprinkle brown sugar on top.

CHOC CHIP COOKIES

125g margarine
60ml sugar
125ml brown sugar
1 egg
250ml gluten-free flour
125ml potato flour
½ teaspoon salt
¾ cup choc tree chips (parev)
½ cup chopped pecan nuts

Preheat oven to 180°C.
Cream butter and sugar, add egg and beat again.
Add rest of ingredients and roll into balls.
Press down with fork.
Bake for 12 – 15 minutes until brown.

AMISH SAND TARTS

500g margarine
4 eggs
2 cups sugar
6 cups flour
pinch salt

Mix butter and sugar.
Add eggs and dry ingredients. Mix well.
Roll and cool in refrigerator.
Slice and bake at 180°C until brown.
Sprinkle with cinnamon and sugar.

DATE PECAN PUMPKIN SQUARES

2½ cups gluten-free flour
1½ teaspoons baking powder
3/4 teaspoon cinnamon
½ teaspoon nutmeg
½ teaspoon cloves
½ teaspoon salt
1 tablespoon margarine
2 cups brown sugar
1 cup cooked mashed pumpkin
2 eggs
vanilla
2 cups dates
1½ chopped pecan nuts

Cream butter and sugar.
Beat in eggs one at a time.
Beat in pumpkin, vanilla and ¼ cup water.
Sift dry ingredients in the bowl.
Toss the dates into the mixture.
Stir in remaining flour mixture, date mixture and pecans until all is well mixed together.
Bake at 180°C for one hour or until tester comes out clean.
Allow to cool and cut into squares.
Serve with ice cream.

Bread

Tips for Baking your Own Bread

I must reiterate the necessity to replace the carbohydrate content in your diet and not only to eliminate the gluten.

As your gluten-free diet becomes more familiar you will need to find ways to simplify your life and your baking routine. I bake four loaves at a time. One loaf is eaten fresh, one is cooled, sliced and oven dried for melba toast, one is made into rusks, and one is sliced and frozen. This will set you ahead with your meals. The frozen bread can be utilised for toast or toasted sandwiches or even for making croutons for soup.

I suggest that on Sunday night you prepare all your ingredients and set up your electric mixer. On Monday morning bake your bread and it's done for the week.

Imagine starting a blue Monday with a crisp crust of your lovely fresh bread.

For lengthy storage remember to slice baked bread before freezing.

FLOUR

Flours with the gluten removed have lost their stretchy viscous factor and therefore gluten-free products cannot imitate the springy moist look of a wheat product. In order to produce something tasty and less crumbly, we need to add some form of protein, either egg, ricotta cheese, or shortening. Flours without gluten work better in combinations, so prepare a flour bin with 2 parts potato flour, 2 parts rice flour and 2 parts gluten-free flour. The addition of soya flour can be regarded as the necessary protein content.

Gluten-free bread tends to be very crumbly, as the gluten is the binding agent. Collect all crumbs and refrigerate as these are very useful in hamburgers, bobotie or even as a topping for casseroles.

The disadvantage of gluten-free flours is that baked foods look pale and unappetising and you have to use a little imagination. Brown them either by brushing with egg or oil.

Southbakels supply a wheat flour with the gluten removed. This is sold as a breadmix and is available at most health stores. This is the flour I refer to as gluten-free in my recipes. Other flours can be added for extra nutrition eg: Rice flour, or potato flour.

My bread recipe is made with this ready made breadmix but I still add a raising agent and other ingredients to the mixture. Your gluten-free mixture should look thinner than the normal bread mixture, almost like thick cream.

Southbakels produce two kinds of gluten-free flour: High protein GF flour which is basically used for people on a gluten-free diet resulting from a coeliac condition, or Dermatitis Herpetiformis. This product contains skim milk. The low protein gluten-free flour does not contain milk and is recommended for coeliacs with a lactose intolerance, or people with renal disease. (See section on Specialist Suppliers.)

'GOOD-LOOKING' GLUTEN-FREE BREAD

500ml gluten-free flour
10ml sugar
10ml baking powder
2 eggs
15ml oil
250ml sparkling water (mineral or soda)

Combine the ingredients in a bowl. Place in a small baking tin lined with tin foil. Glaze with beaten egg, and sprinkle with sesame or poppy seed. Bake in a preheated oven at 180° C for 40 minutes.

QUICK LIGHT BREAD

3 cups gluten-free flour
2 cups water or rooibos tea
¼ cup oil
1 tablespoon sugar
Salt to taste
½ cup sesame seeds (optional)

Mix all ingredients together (mixture should be creamy).
Line a baking tin with foil and coat with oil or cooking spray.
Bake at 180° C for four minutes.

HOT DOG ROLLS

This is a good recipe if you are travelling or going out for a meal and taking your own food along.

3 cups gluten-free bread mix (Southbakels)
1 cup water
1 heaped teaspoon baking powder
1 egg
pinch salt
sesame seed

Mix all ingredients together. There is a special baking tray available for making rolls. Pour mixture into this pan, sprinkle with sesame seed and bake in a medium oven until edges begin to brown.

MUESLI LOAF

2 cups mealie meal
1 cup gluten-free flour
3 tablespoons margarine
1 cup poppy seed
1 cup chopped pecans
3 tablespoons brown sugar
250g dried apricots
2 eggs
1 cup apple juice
2 teaspoons baking powder

Melt apricots in butter with apple juice. Add to other dry ingredients. Beat eggs separately and add to mixture. The mixture must be like thick yoghurt. If too thick add more apple juice.
Bake in a medium oven for 35 mins at 180°.
Wonderfully nutritious start to the day.

'POLENTA' BROWN BREAD

1 cup yellow maize meal
1 cup buckwheat flour
1½ cups gluten-free flour
1 tablespoon sugar
1 teaspoon baking powder
1 teaspoon nutmeg
½ cup sesame
4 tablespoons margarine
1 cup water
4 eggs

Melt margarine. Add to dry ingredients, but add sesame seed last.
Beat eggs on high till well mixed but not for too long and add to mixture.
Bake at 180° C for one hour and serve warm.

MEALIE BREAD (By courtesy of the Angela Day Kitchen)

3 cups minced green mealie kernels
1 teaspoon oil
1 tablespoon sugar
2½ teaspoons gluten-free baking powder
1 tablespoon melted butter
1 beaten egg

Do not use mealies that are too green.
Cut kernels from cob and mince enough to fill three cups.
Combine mealies salt, sugar and baking powder.
Stir in melted butter and egg. Mix well.
Pour the mixture into a greased baking dish and cover with silver foil.
Steam in a pan with water ⅔ up the side of the dish for 1½ – 2 hours.
Serve with hot butter.
To use as a pudding, add raisins and serve with honey or hot jam sauce.

FRANK'S FOCCACIA BREAD

250g gluten-free flour
75g instant yeast
25g sugar
pinch salt
¼ cup olive oil

Dissolve yeast in a little water with sugar.
Pour into flour and salt.
Rest for 10 minutes.
Roll out and shape (flattish).
Brush with olive oil and sprinkle with fresh herbs and salt.
Bake at 180° C for 15 minutes until brown, then turn over and cook for further five minutes. Slice and serve warm.

CHEDDAR BREAD

1½ cups gluten-free flour
1 cup yellow mealie meal
salt to taste
1½ cups milk
1 large cup grated cheese

Rub cheese into dry ingredients and then add milk.
Bake in small loaf tin lined with foil paper.
Sprinkle additional cheese on top and bake at 400° for 25 to 30 minutes.

If you are not into baking yourself, help is at hand.
Excellent gluten-, lactose- and sucrose-free soya bread, polenta bread, carob, corn and coconut muffins, as well as cakes and birthday cakes are manufactured by Mrs Bread-Care.
(See 'What to Buy' section of this book.)

Snacks and Starters

POTATO FRITTERS

2 large potatoes
½ onion
60ml flour
1 egg
5ml baking powder
1ml salt

Grate onion and potato together.
Then add other ingredients and mix well.
Heat oil in pan and drop spoonfuls of the potato mixture into the hot oil.
Fry until golden brown and serve with cream cheese or cinnamon and sugar.

AUBERGINE FRITTERS

(Quantities will vary depending on the number of people being catered for.)

Aubergines
Rice flour
Pepper
Origanum
Oil

Slice the aubergines thinly.
Cover slices with salt and leave to sweat on a board for approximately ½ hour.
Wash and pat dry.
Dip in beaten egg and then in rice flour which has been sprinkled with origanum.
Fry gently till brown and crisp.

CRISPY ONION RINGS

Slice 4 onions thickly
½ cup rice flour
½ cup Gram flour
garlic salt
black pepper

Do not eat onion rings at a steak house as these will be coated in batter made with regular flour.

Heat oil for deep frying.
Add onions to dry flour and seasoning and mix well.
Add ½ cup water.
Mix until batter becomes thick and sticky.
Drop spoonfuls into the heated oil and turn when brown.
Ensure that the rings are well cooked inside and serve to accompany grills or with a dip.

MASHED POTATO PANCAKES

2 cups mashed potato
1 large egg lightly beaten
6 tablespoons gluten-free flour
1½ teaspoons grated onion
1½ teaspoons marjoram
⅓ cup chopped or powdered biltong/bacon (optional – can be used as part of the mix or as a topping)

Mix all ingredients in deep heavy-bottomed frying pan and fry on both sides until golden brown.
Serve warm.
Can be used as a snack or starter or to accompany a main course.

CAULIFLOWER SOUFFLÉ

1kg frozen cauliflower
30g butter
50g Maizena
250ml milk
½ teaspoon salt
3 eggs separated
dash lemon pepper
1 chopped tomato (optional)

Cook the cauliflower in salted water, drain and keep aside.
Melt butter.
Blend in the Maizena.
Add the milk, salt and tomatoes.
Heat and stir slowly until thickened.
Beat the egg yolks until lemon coloured and stir into the cooled white sauce.
Add the cauliflower.
Beat the egg whites until stiff and fold into the cauliflower mixture.
Pour into a buttered casserole dish and bake at 120°C for 30 minutes.
Serve hot.

CHEESE STRAWS

4 tablespoons margarine
1 cup grated cheese
4 tablespoons flour
salt
2 tablespoons tomato sauce

Cream margarine until soft.
Add the cheese and tomato sauce.
Add flour slowly and work in well.
Knead dough on lightly floured board.
Roll out and cut into strips.
Brush top with milk and place in a medium oven until brown.

SUNDAY NITE SUPPER

1 slice gluten-free bread
1 cup grated cheese
1 egg

Mix beaten egg with cheese
Spread thickly on buttered bread.
Add a touch of pepper and grill until brown.
Serve hot with soup.

RICE CHEESE PUFFS

230g boiled rice
90g grated cheese
2 teaspoons gluten-free baking powder
8 tablespoons gluten-free flour
2 well-beaten egg yolks
125ml milk
2 stiffly beaten egg whites
Sunflower oil for frying

Mix rice in a bowl with the cheese, baking powder, flour, egg yolks, salt, pepper and milk.
Fold in the egg whites.
Form into balls and fry in hot oil until golden brown.
Drain on absorbent paper and serve with salad.

CAULIFLOWER BURGERS (VEGETARIAN)

1 cauliflower
2 large potatoes
½ teaspoon mustard (Colmans)
½ teaspoon cumin
1 chopped onion
¼ teaspoon cayenne
2 teaspoons gluten-free flour

Boil cauliflower and potatoes separately.
Drain and cool.
Mash potatoes and chop in cauliflower.
Heat 2 tablespoons of oil and fry the onions, cayenne, mustard and cumin for 2 – 3 mins.
Add to the gluten-free flour.
Divide into patties and refrigerate until ready to deep-fry.
Garnish with coriander.

GEFILTE FISH

(Traditional Jewish Stuffed Fish)

(Very useful. Can be eaten warm or cold and can be stored for a few days if refrigerated.)

1kg deboned stock fish or hake
3 carrots
1 onion
1 potato boiled
salt, pepper
2 eggs

Save the fish bones and boil for an hour to make a stock.
Strain and add the sliced carrots.
Mince filleted fish and add potato, salt and pepper.
Fry onions in oil and add to fish mixture.
Fold in eggs and 1 cup water.
Make small balls of fish and add the strained stock with the carrots.
Simmer for 1½ hours.
Place the fish balls in a table-ready casserole.
Pour the liquid over to cover and refrigerate.

GLUTEN-FREE 'KNEIDLACH'

(Traditional Jewish Dumpling)

1 sachet Telma Potato Pancake mix
2 tablespoons gluten-free flour
2 eggs (separated)
cinnamon powder

Mix all dry ingredients with 200ml cold water, two egg yolks and 1 teaspoon cinnamon.
Beat the egg whites, add to mixture and drop spoonfuls into salt water for about 20 minutes.
Can be served as a vegetable with a main course, but traditionally served in clear chicken soup.

GLUTEN-FREE BOBOTIE

3 bananas sliced
3 tomatoes
3 onions
½ cup seedless raisins
2 tablespoons oil
3 – 4 cups cooked samp
1 beaten egg
½ cup milk
salt and pepper
1 tablespoon curry powder
½ teaspoon cayenne pepper
1 tablespoon vinegar
1 cup minced meat

Braise the onions in oil.
Mince together the raisins, tomatoes and samp.
Pour vinegar over banana.
Mix the ingredients together and pour into a prepared casserole dish.
Mix egg and milk together and pour over casserole.
Bake until brown in a medium oven for about 40 minutes.

SWEETCORN SOUFFLÉ

2 well-beaten eggs
1 cup milk
1 tin sweetcorn (Koo is gluten-free)

Place all ingredients in a buttered casserole dish.
Cut lumps of butter and top with grated cheese.
Bake at 175°C. Serve hot.

Cereals are an important source of Vitamin B, folic acid and fibre. Combine fruit, raisins and sunflower seeds and make your own gluten-free muesli. This can be used as a late night snack or a top-up during the day and is a useful source of energy.

GLUTEN-FREE MUESLI

1 cup corn flakes
1 cup chopped dried applies
1 cup chopped nuts
1 cup raisins
1 cup flaked coconut

Mix all the ingredients well and store in a glass jar with sealed top or a cereal crisper.
Serve with honey and yoghurt.

Rice cakes are a gluten-free life-saver. They are versatile, rich in fibre, travel well and are available in most places. Make sure that they do not have oats added into them – check labels.

Vital rice cakes are the perfect substitute for bread, biscuits and crackers and are completely gluten-free. They are suitable for toddlers.

One can prepare a wonderful array of snacks to take along when invited to a cocktail party where you may not be able to eat any of the snacks offered, as they are generally on wheat-containing crackers or bread.

Suggested gluten-free toppings for rice cakes:
egg mayonnaise
cold meats
hoummous
tahina
Peck's Anchovette
cream cheese and cucumber
cream cheese and smoked salmon
mashed sardines
smoked snoek
chopped egg with onion
salmon with asparagus
Serve on a bed of lettuce and garnish with potato crisps.

RICE CAKE PIZZA

Place two slices of cheese onto a rice cake and spoon tomato sauce over the cheese.
Add sliced olives and anchovies and sprinkle with chopped parsley.
Grill until the cheese melts and bubbles.

Recently available on the market are **carob coated rice cakes** manufactured by Key 4 Health Products. These look and taste good and contain no caffeine. They are an ideal substitute for chocolate snacks and useful for children's outings and school lunches.

The carob-coated mini bars are available in the following flavours:
peanut and raisin
muesli
sunflower seed
peanut
coconut
plain carob

Main Courses

A CURRY PARTY

This is an easy and most economical way to entertain.
You can safely serve:

poppadums (made from lentil flour – there are some available in packets at supermarkets but check labels please)
Mrs Ball's chutney
Wellington's chutney
Ina Paarman's mustards or curry basting
coconut
raisins
sliced banana
tomato and onions
sweet pickles

Check your spice ingredients very carefully to ensure they are gluten-free. Some spices are bulked with flour. Once you have established which spices are safe, always keep to those brands.

CHICKEN CURRY

chicken breasts
onions
Osem chicken soup powder (available at most supermarkets).
Your own home-made chicken stock can also be used.
2 tablespoons ginger
2 tablespoons cumin
3 tablespoons tumeric
2 tablespoons garam masala
1 tablespoon sugar

Dip the chicken in gluten-free rice flour.
Brown quickly in hot oil and place in casserole dish.
Brown the onions in a pot with oil.
Add the spices, sugar, soup powder and a little water.
Bring to the boil and add 1 tablespoon Maizena dissolved in ½ cup water.
Pour over the chicken breasts and bake until soft.
If you use stock often, prepare a large amount of chicken stock, cool and freeze into ice cubes. This is handy for adding to your casseroles, as some commercial stocks do contain gluten.
READ YOUR LABELS.

LÖTTE'S PICKLED FISH

1 kg hake
1 cup vinegar
1 cup water
¾ cup sugar
2 tablespoons tumeric
2 tablespoons pickling spices
1 tablepoon peppercorns
6 bay leaves
sliced onions

Fry fish in egg and mealie meal. Boil together all spices and onions until the onions are yellow. Pour the liquid over the fish and refrigerate for 2-3 days to allow for pickling. Serve cold.

Chinese Food

Chinese food in a restaurant is difficult if you are on a gluten-free diet. It is preferable to make your own at home. It is usually safe to order take-away fried rice from the restaurant.

SWEET AND SOUR SAUCE

½ cup vinegar
1 cup canned pineapple juice
2 tablespoons oyster sauce
3 teaspoons tomato sauce
½ cup sugar
2 tablespoons Maizena dissolved in ½ cup water
Can or jar of chinese pickles
Tin of bamboo shoots

Combine vinegar and pineapple juice in a saucepan, bring to the boil and add tomato sauce, oyster sauce, sugar and Maizena until sauce thickens. Lastly add the pickles and shoots.

TOFU WITH OYSTER SAUCE

Tofu (soya bean curd – available from most health and chinese shops)
3 sticks celery
8 spring onions
1 red pepper
125g mushrooms
2 tablespoons oyster sauce (Amoy)
1 tablespoon dry sherry
2 tablespoons Maizena dissolved in ½ cup water
2 tablespoons oil

Heat the oil. Toss the cubed tofu in oil until browned with shallots, peppers and celery. Add other ingredients until the sauce thickens and serve immediately.

LEMON SAUCE FOR FISH OR CHICKEN

½ cup lemon juice
chicken stock
2 tablespoons Maizena
2 tablespoons honey
3 tablespoons brown sugar
1 tablespoon grated green ginger
1½ cups water

Combine lemon juice, soup stock, Maizena, honey, brown sugar, ginger and water in a saucepan. Stir over low heat until sauce thickens.

FRIED RICE

3 cups chicken soup
3 tablespoons oil
1 cup cooked rice
1 teaspoon sale
½ sliced cucumber
250g mushrooms
250g bacon
1 tin peas
2 onions
1 tablespoon Worcestershire sauce

Slice the cucumbers and mushrooms thinly. Brown with onions. Grill bacon well and crush. Add additional oil. Then add peas, rice and Worcestershire sauce to the heated oil and serve Chinese style.

CINDY'S STICKY CHICKEN WITH CRISPY NOODLES

1 340ml tin Coke
275g gluten-free tomato sauce
275g gluten-free chutney
90g Lazenby's Worcestershire sauce
8 chicken breasts cut into chunks
tin of sliced water chestnuts

Mix the sauce in a bowl. Place the chicken and chestnuts in a lightly oiled dish and pour the sauce over. Sprinkle with sesame seeds and bake for 1½ hours at 180°C.

CRISPY FRIED NOODLES

Heat the oil in a saucepan and dunk spoonfuls of thick chinese rice noodles quickly in and out of the oil before they become brown.

Place around the edge of a large serving dish. Garnish with chopped spring onions and serve your chicken in the centre of the noodles.

NOODLE PUDDING

2 cups of any gluten-free noodles (cooked)
1 cup raisins
¾ cup cottage cheese
1 cup brown sugar
cinnamon to taste

Mix ingredients and pour into buttered casserole dish.
Bake in oven until crisp and brown.

GLUTEN-FREE MEAT LOAF

½ kg minced beef
1 cup cooked rice
pinch salt
pepper to taste
½ onion, finely chopped
1 egg
½ cup tomato juice
parsley

Mix all ingredients together well and turn into loaf pan, lined with paper.
Bake at 175°C for 1hour.

Variations to 1 cup cooked rice:
½ cup crushed pineapple
½ cup crushed corn flakes
1 cup finely grated carrots
or encase the loaf in savoury pastry and bake for special occasions.

GLUTEN-FREE BOBOTIE

Never eat Bobotie away from home as most recipes contain bread.

2 onions, chopped and sauteéd
1 grated apple
30g margarine
500g minced boiled chicken
2 boiled sweet potatoes
60ml milk or Orley Whip
1 tablespoon cayenne pepper powder (Buffalo is gluten-free)
15ml vinegar
5ml turmeric (Buffalo is gluten-free)
2 eggs
dash lemon juice
dash Worcestershire sauce

Pakco masala and curry powder are not suitable for a gluten-free diet.

Combine the ingredients, excluding turmeric and 1 egg and place in baking dish.
Bake for 35 minutes at 180°C.
Beat a second egg with turmeric dissolved in a cup of milk
(or clear soup)
Pour into the baking dish.
Bake until set.

Fat-free Recipes

If you have chronic diarrhoea after your initial diagnosis, you should try to keep to a fat-free diet until your system adjusts and your digestion settles down. Below are three easy recipes to start with.

VEAL AND APPLE DINNER

1 chopped onion
450g lean veal
2 teaspoons tomato purée
2ml chicken stock
4 cooking apples

Brown the meat and onions in Spray & Cook.
Peel, core and slice apples into rings.
Place in a casserole dish with the apples, add the chicken stock and tomato purée and cook at 180°C until tender.
Serve with rice.

CHICKEN CUTLETS

(A good recipe to store in the deep-freeze for quick meals)

1 cooked chicken
2 teaspoons chopped parsley
3 boiled potatoes
1 egg

Mince all the ingredients together.
Add beaten egg and mix well
Shape into rounds and store neatly between layers of wax paper in a plastic container, using as required. Do not defrost.
Fry slowly using Spray & Cook until golden brown on both sides.

SOLE WITH APPLE

Baby dressed soles
cored and sliced apples
clear apple Liquifruit

Grill soles on both sides for a few minutes.
Add a little apple juice to the pan to keep the soles from drying out.
Add apple rings and seasoning to taste and allow to simmer slowly until cooked through.

GLUTEN-FREE STUFFING

250g cooked rice
500g mince
2 tablespoons oil
large onion
celery
parsley
½ cup chopped mushrooms
½ cup chopped pecan nuts
1½ litres chicken stock

Steam rice in a colander until soft.
Brown the onions, mushrooms and mince.
Add to the stock and simmer until the stock is absorbed.
Allow to cool before stuffing turkey.

CHICKEN STUFFING

1 tablespoon chicken fat (Schmaltz)
250g cooked cold rice
1 chopped onion
parsley
lemon pepper and herbs for seasoning
1 tablespoon lemon juice
1 tablespoon potato flour (optional)
1 teaspoon chopped green pepper
1 cup coarsely grated carrots

Brown onions.
Mix all ingredients together.
Allow to cool.
Stuff chicken.

CHESTNUT STUFFING FOR CHICKENS

chestnuts
mixed herbs
garlic
2 tablespoons margarine
small tin peas

Boil the chestnuts and remove shells.
Mince the ingredients together and mix with margarine.
Stuff chicken and roast slowly.

LENTIL STEW

250g red lentils
220g beef mince
1 tin tomato purée
Aromat seasoning
garlic to taste

Soak lentils overnight, boil in clean water until soft and keep separate.
Add tomato purée and garlic to beef mince and simmer gently.
When cooked, add lentils and seasoning.

HOME-MADE NOODLES

8 tablespoons gluten-free flour
5 tablespoons cornflour
2 tablespoons skim-milk powder
1 egg
pinch salt

Mix all ingredients into a dough.
Work with hands and then roll dough as thinly as possible.
Allow to dry out. (Leave for a few hours.)
Cut into thin strips or shapes as desired.
When completely dry store in an airtight Consul jar.
To use cook in salted boiling water.
In an elimination diet the egg can be omitted and replaced with 3 tablespoons water.

VEGETARIAN CABBAGE BAKE

2 cups cooked rice
1 cabbage
3 chopped tomatoes
2 chopped onions
1 tablespoon chopped parsley
1 tin peas
oil
1 teaspoon cumin
black pepper

Separate whole cabbage leaves and place in a bowl of boiling water.
If stems are too thick, slice away part of the stem first.
Soak until soft and cool.
Mix together the rice and peas.
Place 1 tablespoon of the rice mixture into each cabbage leaf.
Roll up leaf and flap ends closed and then secure with a toothpick.
Place in buttered casserole dish.
Cover with tomatoes, onions, parsley and cumin.
Add enough vegetable stock to poach the parcels.
Cook for 35 minutes at 180°C.

POTATO PUDDING

8 potatoes
1 onion
3 tablespoons gluten-free flour
2 tablespoons oil
2 eggs
salt and pepper
1kg mince
3 tomatoes
Aromat seasoning
gluten-free soya sauce

Grate potatoes and onion.
Sprinkle with flour to prevent discolouring.
Brown the mince and seasoning and set aside.
Mix other ingredients into the potato mixture and pour into a greased dish – one layer of potato, then a layer of mince and a layer of potato on top.
Bake for 60 minutes at 180°C.

HOUMMOUS SAUCE

1 cup chick peas (cooked or tinned)
garlic
½ cup lemon juice
1 cup milk
parsley
salt
Aromat seasoning

Mix all ingredients in a liquidiser, adding the milk last.
The sauce must have a creamy consistency.

Delightful Desserts

If you are stuck for a gluten-free birthday cake, here is a foolproof quick answer

ICE CREAM CAKE

2 litres vanilla ice cream
3 peppermint crisps (check brands)
Hershey's chocolate sauce
Bottled cherries, green and red

Allow ice cream to soften to a mixing texture. Crush the peppermint crisps and add to ice cream and chopped cherries. Pour chocolate sauce into a shaped mould. Spoon the ice cream over the sauce and re-freeze. When ready to serve unmould onto a large plate. Add cream decoration and candles and surround with little chocolates or marshmallows.

ANN'S MACHON CAKE

(Wonderful dessert for dinner parties)

Meringues
4 egg whites
80 g castor sugar
80 g ground almonds
Spread onto two baking sheets in a circle, not too thinly and bake until just brown.

Filling

2 egg whites
150 g sugar
150 g margarine
90 g cocoa
1 slab Nestlé Albany

Beat all ingredients together in a double boiler and then place between the layers of meringue and decorate.

LEMON MERINGUE PIE

Crumble gluten-free biscuits to make base (eg Liga biscuits)

Meringue

28g sugar
28g castor sugar
2 egg whites

Filling

Juice and rind of 2 lemons
1 tablespoon cornflour
1 tablespoon oil
Water
2 egg yolks
55g sugar

Squeeze juice of 2 lemons, then add enough water to make 6 tablespoons of liquid. Blend with the cornflour. Put oil in a pot and add the mixture. Add 55g sugar and lemon rind. Cook steadily, stirring to avoid lumps until thick and smooth. Remove from heat and beat in 2 egg yolks. Place in moderate oven for 15 minutes. Whisk egg whites until very stiff. Add sugar to whites slowly, a teaspoon at a time. Bake again in very low oven 135°C for 1 hour.

BANANA TART

4 sesame seed bars
6 ripe bananas
Small tin condensed milk
½ cup orange juice

Crumble sesame seed bars and make a base. Boil bananas and orange juice together until soft. Mix well until smooth. Remove from the stove. Add the condensed milk, stirring well, and allow to set. Garnish with cream.

WAFFLES

4 tablespoons rice flour
2 tablespoons sugar
2 eggs
¾ cup juice or water

Heat a waffle iron and coat with oil or cooking spray. Spoon mixture onto iron. Do not open until golden brown. Serve immediately.

SMOOTH CHOCOLATE MAHOGANY SAUCE (for ice cream)

35g Nestlé cocoa
60g Butterscotch Schnapps
250ml water
60g Cardin or Olé margarine
230g sugar
30g Maizena

Add water and Maizena to all dry ingredients. Heat slowly until the mixture begins to thicken. Add the margarine. Keep stirring for another minute and pour into a bowl. Serve with chunks of pineapple and lemon sorbet.

LACTOSE-FREE FUDGE

450g Besan or Gram flour
225g margarine (Cardin or Olé)
225g sugar
1½ teaspoons cinnamon
1 teaspoon vanilla essence
50g chopped nuts

Melt the margarine and add the gram flour. Reduce to low heat and cook for 12-15 minutes, stirring all the time. Add other ingredients. Allow to cool. Roll into balls. Roll in finely chopped almonds and store in an airtight container.

MAPLE AND WALNUT SAUCE

60g margarine
80ml maple syrup
15ml brown sugar
1 sachet Orley Whip
Walnuts

Place the margarine, syrup and sugar in a saucepan and stir over a low heat until sugar is dissolved. Continue to stir until it is syrupy. Remove from heat and cool slightly. Stir in Orley Whip and chopped walnuts.
Can be used over ice cream, steamed pudding, waffles, etc.

CHINESE NOODLE PUDDING

Rice noodles are available from good health stores or from Sui Hing Hong in Commissioner Street, Johannesburg. Ensure that the noodles you purchase are rice noodles and do not contain wheat.

100g plain rice noodles
50g sugar
25g sultanas
½ teaspoon nutmeg
½ teaspoon ground cardamom
300ml water
50g margarine
Almonds

Separate the noodles to loosen. Fry sultanas in margarine until soft. Add almonds. When brown add noodles and fry quickly. Simmer the fried mixture in the water mixed with sugar until liquid is absorbed. Garnish with a few chopped maraschino cherries and cream if you wish.

DEVASTATING WAFER FUDGE

1 packet Gluten-Ex biscuits
500g icing sugar
3 tbsp cocoa
2 eggs
1 teaspoon vanilla essence
300g margarine or peanut butter

Place biscuits into a plastic bag and crush with rolling pin.
Melt butter over a low heat and add icing sugar and vanilla. Stir well. Add crushed biscuits to mixture and spread onto oiled baking sheet and cool in fridge. Cut into squares and ration among family and friends!

PINEAPPLE TART

1 grated pineapple
2 apples coarsely grated
1 tablespoon sugar
½ teaspoon lemon juice
1 tablespoon cornflour

Crumble gluten-free biscuits to form base.
Stir all ingredients over a low heat until thickened and pour onto crumb crust.
Garnish with extra crumbs and allow to cool.

MELKTERT

4½ cups skim milk
2½ tablespoons Maizena
1 cup sugar
Pinch salt
3 eggs
2½ tablespoons gluten-free flour
1 teaspoon vanilla essence
1 tablespoon butter

Tart base

500g crushed gluten-free biscuits or Kellogg's crumbs
3 tablespoons margarine
2 tablespoons sugar

Melt margarine, add sugar and crumbs and press into buttered tart dish.
To make a more interesting base you can add coconut, chopped almonds or sesame seed to the crumbs.

Filling

Let milk boil. Beat eggs and sugar until creamy. Add to sugar, cornflour, flour and salt. Mix well. Pour boiling milk onto this mixture and stir thoroughly. Return to stove until mixture thickens. Add vanilla and butter and pour into dish. Sprinkle with cinnamon. (If the mixture becomes lumpy on thickening, stir well off the stove or beat with a mixer.)

KOEKSISTERS

4g dried yeast
½ cup warm milk
1 tablespoon melted butter
Pinch salt
¾ cup sugar
2 cups gluten-free flour
1 teaspoon cinnamon
2 eggs beaten well

Dissolve the yeast in the milk and stir in the butter and salt. Sift together flour, sugar and cinnamon and add half to yeast mixture. Add the eggs, then the remaining flour mixture. Knead well on floured board. Roll out dough to 2cms thick. Shape into rounds and allow to rise until double in bulk. Drop into hot fat, raised side down. Fry until lightly brown. Drain on absorbent paper. Dust with a mixture of sugar and cinnamon. Serve with jam or cream.

CRUNCHY APPLE TART

Crunchy topping (recipe below)
4 tablespoons butter
¾ cup castor sugar
2 egg yolks
1 cup corn flakes

Melt butter and sift in dry ingredients. Combine to make a smooth dough and line a pie plate. Spread with a thin layer of apricot jam.

Filling

Cook apples with water and sugar until tender. Mix with currants and spoon into pie plate. (Quantity depends on the number of people you wish to feed.)

Crunchy Topping

Cream butter and sugar. Mix in egg yolks and beat well. Stir in corn flakes but not too vigorously. Top the apple tart with this mixture and bake in preheated oven at 230°C for 30 minutes.

CUSTARD

1 egg
1½ cups skim milk
4 teaspoons sugar
1 teaspoon gluten-free flour or Maizena
½ teaspoon vanilla essence

Separate the egg. Beat the egg yolk with half a cup of milk. Add the remaining cold milk slowly. Mix sugar, gluten-free flour and salt. Combine the two mixtures and cook in a double boiler until thick and no taste of the starch remains. Remove from heat and add vanilla essence.

PANCAKES

1 cup gluten-free flour
1 egg
1 tablespoon sugar
1½ cups milk or Rice Dream
2 tablespoons margarine
Oil for frying

Make a well in the flour and add egg and milk. Stir in melted butter. Allow to stand for ½ hour as this will produce a lighter pancake. Fry in a minimal amount of oil until golden brown on both sides.

ALMOND PANCAKES

2 eggs
225ml milk
½ teaspoon vanilla essence
1 tablespoon melted butter
125g gluten-free flour
30g castor sugar
1 tablespoon ground almonds

Beat the liquids well. Add to the dry ingredients. Mix till smooth and leave to stand for 30 minutes.

CORNMEAL PANCAKES

½ cup mealie meal
½ cup boiling water
3 eggs
½ cup potato flour
2 tablespoons butter
¾ cup milk or Rice Dream

Pour mealie meal into a bowl and add boiling water. Stir till smooth. Allow to cool slightly. Add eggs, melted butter, flour and other ingredients. Cover and allow batter to stand for one hour. Mix again before making pancakes.

Specialist Suppliers

POSTSCRIPT

Coeliac Survey

The provision of facilities for coeliac disease are very poor in this country. In order to improve the situation we need information and statistics regarding the number of affected people and their adaptation to a gluten-free diet.

Please complete the survey questionnaire and post to:

Carole Smollan
134 – 10th Avenue
Highlands North
2192

Tel: (011) 885-2020
Fax: (011) 440-9836

SURVEY OF GLUTEN-FREE DIET IN SOUTHERN AFRICA

Name: ....

Address: ....

....

Telephone: .... Fax: ....

1 Age of person on a gluten-free diet

....

2 Are you currently on a gluten-free diet?

....

3 How long have you been on the diet?

....

4 Have you had an intestinal biopsy? By whom?

....

5 Is your diagnosis via a hospital or a private doctor?

....

6 What are your main symptoms after eating gluten-containing products?

....

....

7 From which country do your ancestors originate?

....

8 Is there more than one member of your family with gastro-intestinal problems?

....

9 Where do you buy your gluten-free supplies?

....

....

10 What product would you particularly like available?

....

11 Would you buy imported gluten-free biscuits if they were available?

....

12. Do you maintain a gluten-free diet for reasons other than a gluten allergy?

....

13 Are you aware of any other patient on a gluten-free diet?

....

14 Would you be interested in seeing a video on Coeliac Disease?

....

15 How did you originally hear about *The Gluten-Free Guide for Southern Africa*?

....

16 If you would like to, please write a short description of how you feel and how you manage your gluten-free diet when travelling, baking, or eating out, etc.

....

....

....

....

....

....

....

....

....

....

....

....

....

In order to increase the range of products available on South African shelves and at prices we can afford, we need to put pressure on the government to reduce the surcharge on these gluten-free items.

You can help by writing to me and assisting me in showing that there are numbers of people who need these products for a well-balanced diet.

Our diet is extremely expensive and you are welcome to write to me enclosing a stamped, self-addressed envelope, for an explanation of my tax rebate claim. My address is:

Carole Smollan
134 – 10th Avenue
Highlands North
2192

Useful International Addresses

With special thanks to Tanya and Andrea Smollan for researching these addresses.

Australia

Coeliac Society of Australia
P O Box 22
Chadstoen Centre
Victoria 3148
(Each state has their own society)

Austria

Oesterreichische Arbeitsgemeinschaft Zoliakie
Anton Baumgarten Strasse 44/C5/2302
A-1232 Vienna

Hotel in Austria:
Goldener Adler
Family Kurz
A-6561 Ischgl
Tirol
Tel: 743 5444 5217
Fax: 743 5444 5571

Canada

Canadian Coeliac Society
6519B Mississauga Road
Mississauga
Ontario
LSN1A6

Germany

Deutsche Zoliakie Gesellschaft
Filderhaupt Strasse 61
D-70599 Stuttgart
Tel: 49 711 454514

Holland

Nederlands Coeliac Vereniging
Kerkshaar 28
NL 6883 HT Velp
Tel/Fax: 31 026 363 5362

Hungary

Liszterzenyek Erdekkpviseletenek
Orszagos Egyesulete
Palanta U11
H-1025 Budapest
Tel: 36 1 135 1278

Ireland

Liam Conlan
Coeliac Society of Ireland
4 North Brunswick Street
Dublin 7
Tel: 353 10872 1471

Italy

Associazione Italiana Celiachia
Sezione Lombardia
Via S Senatore 2
20100 Milan
Tel/Fax 0039 2 867820

Malta

Mary Rose Carvana
Coeliac Association, Malta
LUMUT, Upper Gardens
St Juliana STB 05
Tel: 370 778

Spain

Asociacion de Padres de Celiacos de las Palmas
Apdo de Correos 4237
3501 Las Palmas de G/C
Tel: 928 25 31 32

Asociacion de Padres de Celiacos de Madrid
C/Pozas 4° – Local
28004 Madrid
Tel: 91 523 0494
Fax: 91 531 05 49

ACE
Asociacion Celiaca Espanola
Sede Nacional
C/ercilla 19 4° – 3
28005 Madrid
Tel: 91 473 19 67

SMAP
Celiacs de Catalunya
Ronda Universitat 21 8° – F
08007 Barcelona
Tel: 93 317 72 00 ext 282
Fax: 93 412 03 82

(Branches in Cordoba, Palma de Mallorce, Tenerife, Vallencia, Pamplona and many more.)

Sweden

Svenska Celiakie Forbundet
P O Box 1160
17123 Solna

United Kingdom

Coeliac Society of the United Kingdom
P O Box 220
High Wycombe
Bucks HP1 12HY
Tel: 0494 37278

United States of America

Coeliac Disease Foundation
13251 Ventura Blvd.
Suite 3, Studio City
CA 91604 1838
Tel: 818 990 2354

Coeliac Sprue Association
P O Box 31700
Omalia
NE 68131 0700

Notes

NOTES

Notes

Notes

NOTES